Advance Praise for *More*

"*More Time for You* offers a powerful and practic[ ]
in their lives for immediate results."—Jackie Gl[ ]
Senior Director of Human Resources, EMC Corporation

"The principles and practices in *More Time for You* have enabled and inspired our global sales team to produce results far beyond expectations, as we look forward to even greater performance and productivity."—Ray Hollinger, Director, Sales Development, IHS, Inc.

"*More Time for You* has given me a much needed breath of fresh air. As a manager, I knew how to organize at work but was not very effective at balancing my day-to-day life. The techniques and systems the authors share in this book have helped me see that I have the power to get it all done as well as have the time to enjoy life! And these tools are very easy to implement. I wish I could have read it sooner!"—Marla Dillard-Lemons, Quality Systems Manager, Ford Motor Company

"The practices in *More Time for You* have been eagerly embraced by our busy corporate and field-based employees looking for new ways to be productive and focused in both their work and home lives. One of the things our employees found most helpful was learning the habit of capturing everything in one place. For many people the impact was immediate! They were released from the anxiety of worrying about all the things they had to do—wherever they were currently being stored. After implementing this practice, people reported sleeping better, taking more time for exercise, and generally feeling more in control of their lives."—Helen Zarba, Director, Education and Training, Bright Horizons Family Solutions LLC

"When Rosemary and Alesia tried to convince me to consider a new approach to managing tasks and time, I was dubious at best. I am grateful they were so persistent, because their approach has changed my life. I now have peace of mind knowing that my priorities have a place on my calendar, and I need no longer worry about what I might be forgetting to do!"—Elaine Gentile, Leadership & Organization Development Manager, Iron Mountain, Inc.

"Trying to get more done in less time is a challenge we are all facing during these times. Finally—a practical guide that provides readers with a clear roadmap toward increased efficiency. This book will change your life."—Mike Hyter, President and Managing Partner, Global Novations

"A man I admire was once described by one of his peers as a consummate old-school gentleman, 'having time for me at the drop of a hat—he is never hurried, always patient, always willing to listen, and never unavailable.' *More Time for You* is a book that captures relatively easy tools that allow us to be patient, attentive, and available in our lives—on the job, to our loved ones, and in our communities. It embraces today's technology to create room for each of us to live old-school lives.—Stuart Fross, Partner, K&L Gates, LLP

"With a one-hour commute, two brands to manage, a daughter in college on the East Coast, a son in high school on the West Coast, and a wife who signed up for more companionship than I could give, I was spread too thin. I had all the tools but lacked the system to put them to work. *More Time for You* has restored my quality of life. The techniques and tips for achieving greater organization, productivity, and order in life are simple, understandable, and easy to implement."—Pete Worley, Brand President, Teva and Simple Shoes, Deckers Outdoor Corporation

"The African Proverb 'For tomorrow belongs to the people who prepare for it today' captures the thoughtfulness and brilliance in *More Time for You*. We, the people, spend so much of our time wasting it away. As best said by Anne Frank 'How wonderful it is that nobody need wait a single moment before starting to improve the world.' This book gives us the opportunity to regain our time so we can contribute to our world in a more meaningful, creative, productive way!"—Valerie E. Patton, Executive Director, St. Louis Business Diversity Initiative

"Although I've always considered myself an excellent manager of my business and personal schedule, after reading *More Time for You* I now feel that I may have been the victim of an overactive ego. The authors' sage advice, written and laid out in a clear and concise manner, is a refreshing and insightful demonstration of just how easily you can get more out of every day. I know that it made an immediate impact on my daily routine; and it could change your life!"—Michael D. Lyons, Prudential Lyons Group Real Estate

"One trait the happiest and most successful people I know have in common is the rigor and discipline with which they manage their time. While each of us has been given the gift of time, few would say they manage this precious resource wisely and well. This book enables you to set and fulfill your dreams, making time for what's most important to you instead of simply living each day like you're two steps behind on the treadmill of life. It contains the tools successful and fulfilled people use to seize the gift of time with purpose and passion, so they can live their lives with maximum meaning and minimal regrets."—Susan Hodgkinson, Founder and Principal, The Personal Brand Company

"This book brings new insight and clarity to one of the big challenges of modern life: keeping true to oneself while managing—or saying 'no' to the 'stuff' of busy lives. As a parent, spouse, friend, entrepreneur, and cancer survivor, I will look to *More Time for You* again and again. The ideas, tools and thinking of this book will help you move from a life of good intentions to a more intentional life."—Terri Nimmons, Principal and Founder, Stone Lake Leadership Group

"*More Time for You* sets forth a tangible battle plan for conquering the 'Holy Grail' of productivity—how to balance the must do's and have some quality time left for you. Where Covey began the dialogue, Tator and Latson continue the journey toward successful time management, providing the reader with up-to-date strategies and tactics for slaying the 'procrastination dragon' and creating more time for the areas of your life that matter! Whether you report to an office, work remotely, are a student or a homemaker, this book is a must read, providing aspirations of what your life could be and inspiration on how to get there."—Michael Floyd, Founder, CEO, Pharmaffectiv, LLC

(Continued on page 228)

MORE TIME for YOU

**A Powerful System to Organize
Your Work and Get Things Done**

ROSEMARY TATOR and ALESIA LATSON

AMACOM

AMERICAN MANAGEMENT ASSOCIATION
New York • Atlanta • Brussels • Chicago • Mexico City • San Francisco
Shanghai • Tokyo • Toronto • Washington, D.C.

Bulk discounts available. For details visit:
www.amacombooks.org/go/specialsales
Or contact special sales:
Phone: 800-250-5308
E-mail: specialsls@amanet.org
View all the AMACOM titles at: www.amacombooks.org

Library of Congress Cataloging-in-Publication Data

Tator, Rosemary.
    More time for you : a powerful system to organize your work and get
things done / Rosemary Tator and Alesia Latson.
        p.   cm.
    Includes index.
    ISBN-13: 978-0-8144-1647-1
    ISBN-10: 0-8144-1647-0
    1. Time management.   2. Personal information management.   I. Latson,
Alesia.   II. Title.
HD69.T54T38   2011
650.1'1—dc22

                                                            2010021861

About AMA

American Management Association (www.amanet.org) is a world leader in talent
development, advancing the skills of individuals to drive business success. Our mission is
to support the goals of individuals and organizations through a complete range of products
and services, including classroom and virtual seminars, webcasts, webinars, podcasts,
conferences, corporate and government solutions, business books, and research. AMA's
approach to improving performance combines experiential learning—learning through
doing—with opportunities for ongoing professional growth at every step of one's career
journey.

Printing number

10   9   8   7   6   5   4   3   2   1

To Roosevelt Wilson, Linda Wilson, Debra Latson,
and Michael Latson:
Your memory will live forever in my heart.
—ALESIA

To June and John Meehan:
You have inspired me, and thousands of others,
to be all you can be.
—ROSEMARY

CONTENTS

ACKNOWLEDGMENTS

We thank **Claudia Gere** whose dedication, infinite patience, and amazing talent transformed our ideas into a coherent book. She has been our Sherpa in guiding us through the writing and publishing process. Without her uncompromising support this book would not be a reality.

We acknowledge the founders of Mission Control Productivity LLC for contributing to our lifelong inquiry into what it takes to live into our potential, as well as for creating the workshop where we met. We thank Brian Stuhlmuller, who launched Mission Control, and Brian Regnier, who developed many of the concepts and materials. Your coaching of and commitment to our development has made a major difference in our lives. We also appreciate Doug Fisher's collaborative spirit and commitment to partnership.

A very special thanks to our early readers for their invaluable feedback: Debra Baker, Janet Britcher, Bonni Carson DiMatteo, Sue Fraser, Diana Hammer, Bruce Katcher, Marianne Mortara, Vanessa Latson, Rob Phillips, Sarah Phillips, Carol Salloway, Eb Schmidt, Jane Wells, Deborah Wild, and Helen Zarba.

And to Mary Gallagher, who witnessed the conception of this book and was an inspiration to both of us throughout this process.

There are many people who have contributed to the fields of productivity, stress management, and living a purposeful life who have influenced our thinking and to whom we are deeply grateful.

—Rosemary Tator and Alesia Latson, 2010

To Alesia: Your commitment to excellence and your eloquence flows throughout the book. I have thoroughly enjoyed writing this book with you. Our collaboration has added to my life in so many ways, and chief among them is my newfound understanding and appreciation of how wonderfully a committed partnership can work.

To Wes, my husband, my partner in life: It's your steadfast support for me and my endeavors and your ever-present love that sources our wonderful life together. To our children Angel and Seth and their spouses Ian and Erin: I honor your commitment to each other, your dedication to consciously and lovingly parenting our beautiful grandchildren, your pursuit of ongoing growth professionally and spiritually, and how you contribute so selflessly to your communities.

To my parents, June and John Meehan: Your ever-present love, along with your can-do attitude, has given me the foundation to live fully and make a difference. To my siblings Jack, June, Maureen, Michael, Theresa, and Colleen: You, your spouses, and your children have celebrated with me during the best of times as well as those "other" times, and I always know I can count on your love and support.

To my wonderful grandchildren, Kiran, Sam, and Zoe: I am so thankful to be able to have you in my life. Kiran and Zoe, even though we are a continent apart and see each other only a few times each year, you are forever in my thoughts. And, Sam, watching you grow and playing with you, learning from you, and relishing in your glow is always the highlight of my week.

To the members of our Mastering Effectiveness Program—Joe Cicero, Ramona Dorsey, Carol Holland, Ray Hollinger, Rich McAndrew, Dana McIntyre, Andy Miser, and Cathleen Moynihan: Partnering with you was a constant source of inspiration and support as well as a plethora of material for this book.

To my fellow Sufficiency Partners—Jen Cohen, Carol Dearborn, Miriam Hawley, Gina LaRoche, Martha Russell, and Mike Scarpone, as well as my partner, Trudy van de Berg, your "sacred listening" has given rise to my voice.

To my clients, coworkers, and business partners—present and former: You've all played a part in my thought process and experiences. Thank you for your trust and respect.

—Rosemary Tator, 2010

Not only does it take a village to raise a child, but it takes one to write a book as well. I have been blessed with a wonderful village of family, friends, clients, and colleagues who have provided support, guidance, and encouragement along the way.

Chief among them is my coauthor, Rosemary Tator, a wonderful thinking and writing partner. Rosemary, thank you for the coaching and support through the years. Your patience and exuberant spirit brought us through the darkness that accompanies the writing process.

To my fabulous husband, Brian: Thank you for your warm encouragement, divine patience, daily inspiration, and unconditional love. I am so grateful and privileged to have you as my life's companion.

To my parents, Joyce Wilson and Leroy Dockett, thank you for your loving support and guidance and all that you've done in shaping the person that I've become. Thank you to my siblings, Rory Dockett, Robin Wilson, and Arlene Dockett, for putting up with my idiosyncrasies and supporting me in spite of them. To my nieces (Vanessa, Jourdan, and Jada) and nephews (Matthew, Joshua, and Kaleb): You are a source of joy, and true treasures in my life, inspiring and filling me with optimism for the future.

I'm very blessed to have a large extended family of grandparents, aunts, uncles, and cousins who have generously and lovingly contributed to my life. I am forever grateful for your love and unyielding support.

To my enduring supporters, Angela Crowder-Clark, Janet Britcher, Camille Brower, Alicia Cahill-Watts, Tina Campidelli, Sandy Davis, Janice Clements Skelton, Sue Hodgkinson, Marcia Kimm, Katie Lesene, Yvonne Murphy, Terri Nimmons, Patricia Patterson, Jeanne Robison, Linda Rodriguez, Sharon Schneider, Theresa Tillmon, Magda Trujuilo, Henrietta Turnquest, and Cindy Walker: I can't imagine what my life would be without you. Thank you for your unconditional support, dead-on coaching, gut-busting laughter, and for that special sister-friend bond that sustains and nourishes my soul. I dearly cherish you.

I'd be remiss if I didn't also mention my brother-friends who throughout the years have been great and patient mentors, namely, Scott David, Percy Hayles, John Ryan, and Nate Norman.

To my clients and colleagues, thank you for the privilege to work and grow alongside with you. Whatever value you have received from working with me, I've received that, and a thousand times more, from working with you.

—Alesia Latson, 2010

INTRODUCTION

ALESIA'S STORY

The bane of my existence has always been the management (or in my case, the mismanagement) of time. I have struggled with finding time to "do it all." In high school and college, I was notorious for pulling all-nighters to study or write papers (a habit I have not outgrown). When I started my career, I was often the last to leave the office. As a consultant, I am challenged to travel, facilitate workshops, undertake project work, address client needs, prospect for new clients, and write for a living. In addition to nurturing my marriage and caring for my family, there is all the stuff of life: friends, holidays, parties, errands, bills, exercising, piano practice, classes, reading, theater, vacation, thank-you notes, e-mail, tax preparation, and so on. For me, it all can get daunting. I'm embarrassed to tell you how many flights, trains, appointments, and opportunities I've missed. How many times I've run out of gas. How many birthdays, anniversaries, and events that I wanted to attend, but forgot about. How many books and articles I haven't read; movies and plays that I haven't seen; classes that I haven't taken; or trips and sporting events that I haven't enjoyed—not because I didn't have the time (trust me, I've had plenty of time to do these things), but because I didn't *appropriate* the time. I was neither designing my days consciously nor creating my life purposefully. This proven system to organize your work and get things done, the system that Rosemary and I share in this book, is the result of our own experience and exploration into finding a way to manage our busy lives to be fulfilling—not just full of things to do.

Is my life perfect? No. Far from it. Am I late for the occasional meeting or appointment? Yes. Do I do everything I want to do? Not always. But do I have a great life? Yes! Not because I get everything done that I want to do in a day, week, month, or year, but because I've designed it to be full of the stuff of life that means the most to me. And that couldn't happen without the system that we'll introduce to you in this book. So settle in and buckle up. It's going to be a great ride!

—Alesia Latson

ROSEMARY'S STORY

For most of my life, I have taken on more and more projects, events, and things to do than there is time to do them. As soon as I get into a project, I see all these resources and people that could enhance the project, and I add them to my already-bulging schedule. I come by this honestly. I consider myself a "professional multi-tasker" and have been at it since my childhood. As the oldest of seven children, I learned from the best of the best: Back then, multitasking meant finding one child's mittens while sending the other one out the door, while telling my mother, "Everything is all set." And it continued into my career. I hate to admit it, but I actually trained people to hire others based on how well they could multitask.

Adding to my "condition" is my high-energy, upbeat, "I can do it" attitude. At first blush, this characteristic of mine may sound like a great blessing and a benefit in accomplishing things in life. Perhaps it would be, were I in control of it. You see, these qualities affect not only me but other people, too. At times everyone around me is spinning with me at the speed of light. As exciting as this experience may be in the moment, and as great as the "high" may be for pulling things off once again, as my husband says, "Dear, this is totally unsustainable." You can just about predict the forgotten messages, the missed thank-you notes, and the settling for less than what would have been possible if I had been more realistic with my time. My inability to deal with twenty-four hours in a day and 168 hours in a week has been a major cause of angst throughout my life and career.

The processes and practices that Alesia and I share in this book are a direct result of our own experiences, struggles, and triumphs. We not only write about these practices and coach and train people in them, but we live by them, too. This system of practices "grounds me." I face the reality of the time available to me as never before. It supports me in remembering that I truly can only do one thing well at a time. Making choices has become a natural part of my day now, and my reliability has greatly increased. I have the time to focus on what I say is most important. I'm still an optimistic person, but now a much more realistic one also.

As you make your way through the book, try these practices on for size and make them your own. This is your one life.

—Rosemary Tator

PART ONE

SO MUCH TO DO

Know the true value of time; snatch, seize, and enjoy every moment of it . . .

—LORD CHESTERFIELD

1

TIME AND EFFECTIVENESS

Live a good life. And in the end, it's not the years in the life, it's the life in the years.

—ABRAHAM LINCOLN

If you had Aladdin's magic lamp and could make three wishes, it's a good bet one of them would be to have more time. You wouldn't be reading this book right now if you already had all the time you wanted. Chances are that you are interested in having more time *not* just for the sake of having more time (after all, who wants to have more time to be in the dentist chair?). You want more time for particular purposes. You want more time to do all the things you dream about doing. More time for the things you love; more time to spend with friends and family. More time to engage in work that is fulfilling, rewarding, and satisfying. More time to spend in places that you dream about going, or places that you long to return. More time to shop, read, dance, cook, sing, play, sail, travel, paint, listen to music, run, walk, read, sleep, eat, kiss, ski, fish, knit, journal, garden, volunteer, entertain, play golf, meditate, hike, make wine, or swim. More time to enjoy the nectar and sweetness of life.

Unfortunately, there is no way to get more time. We can't manufacture minutes. It's impossible to add more hours to the day. We have a fixed quantity of twenty-four hours in a day to work with. So, it's not how much time we have; it's what we do with the time that we are given.

That's what this book is all about. It's about adding "life in the years," and having compelling answers to the following questions: What will you do with your allocation of time on this planet? Who will you become? What will you have? What legacy will you leave behind?

If you want more time for you, then you are going to need to increase your capacity to be more effective, efficient, and productive with the time you currently have. This book gives you step-by-step instructions on how to do just that.

Our journey begins with the lives of three people who, in juggling the priorities of their professional and personal lives, feel overwhelmed by trying to plan and do all the tasks required for all aspects of their lives. Starting with these stories, this book explains what robs us of our time, and then provides a powerful system for organizing work and getting things done so that there is more time for you to live your life on your own terms.

ELIZABETH'S STORY

Elizabeth is a hardworking, committed wife, mother, and professional who defines herself by how much she is able to accomplish. She knows it is often impossible to complete every task on her daily list, but continues to feel incompetent when she fails to get something done. She finds herself caught in a vicious cycle: The more she struggles to do everything that needs to be done, the more there is for her to do. And the more there is to do, the more dissatisfied she becomes in her role as a wife, mother, and professional.

When Elizabeth began her job as a commercial real estate broker, she was both confident and excited about this new opportunity; nowadays, she finds it difficult to handle the demands of her professional and personal life. A typical day might involve showing the mill property, meeting with the developers for the new school, searching for the tax card for the multifamily house that she's been trying to close for the last two months, catching her son's soccer practice a half hour late, picking up her daughter from Girl Scouts, and making ten calls to organize the bake sale for her church. But no matter how hard she tries, no matter how much she manages to get done, she continues to fall behind.

There are some obvious signs that Elizabeth is in trouble. The first sign is that she has neglected to take care of herself. She fails to exercise or eat nutritiously, so she is overweight. She constantly skips breakfast or lunch to create more work time in her schedule, and is consumed with hunger by the time that she arrives home at 7:30 p.m. When she walks in the door, she is ravenous and eats whatever she can find that is both filling and easy to make. By this time, it is either too late or she is too tired to enjoy her family. Despite her most valiant attempts, she usually falls asleep within fifteen minutes of sitting and relaxing with her husband and children. At 5:00 a.m. the following morning, the alarm jolts her from sleep, and by 6:30 a.m., she begins her commute back to her office, at work once more.

Another sign of trouble is clutter. Elizabeth moves so quickly that she creates a wake of clutter behind her, one wave after another. The accumulating mess becomes so daunting that she cannot bear to face it. She is incapable of sending or receiving e-mail because she has exceeded her storage quota and filled her inbox. She can barely find anything on her desk because of the massive clutter. She has piles of papers on her floor, file cabinet, and every other surface, leaving only the seat of her chair as an available resting place for important documents. Elizabeth has become oblivious to the albatross around her neck. Arms flailing, she is drowning in the waves of responsibilities and clutter, with no hope of rescue.

PHIL'S STORY

To the naked eye, Phil appears to be a successful manager at a computer company. He holds a high-paying position and has an administrative assistant, Rebecca. Unlike Elizabeth in the previous story, Phil has Rebecca nearby to manage the papers, the filing, and the clutter. As his gatekeeper, Rebecca schedules his important personal and work-related appointments and makes sure that people don't interrupt him unnecessarily. With all of this support, you might think Phil would have everything under control.

Phil has three teenage boys and realizes the importance of having more time to spend with his family and being present in the lives of his children. He knows and honors that crucial role he plays as a teacher, role model, and father to his sons. He wants to spend as much time as possible with his boys before they are grown and engaged in their own life endeavors.

One day at work, Phil found himself thinking, "I have to stop this! I need the time to see my children grow up. No matter what, I must stop spending so much of my time at work." Despite these undying pleas to himself, he continued to be consumed by his work.

So he told Rebecca, "Please, make sure I leave work on time."

She replied softly, "I'm not even here when you leave, Phil."

"Well," said Phil, "let's just try not to schedule appointments for me after 5:30 p.m." Rebecca readily agreed. This plan was successful for only two days before Phil fell back into the same trap. He found himself leaving work at seven-thirty or eight o'clock at night.

Disheartened and exhausted, Phil feels defeated. Even with the help of an assistant, he cannot manage his schedule such that he can be home in time to have dinner with his family.

ERIC'S STORY

Eric, a senior vice president of sales for an insurance company, is respected as an energetic leader, an influential member of his community, and a caring father and husband. He attended one of our two-day productivity and effectiveness workshops where we discussed how many seemingly helpful strategies for managing time, such as multitasking, are actually detrimental.

That first evening, Eric went home and took his wife and two children out for ice cream following dinner. He turned his car onto Interstate 91, the same busy road that he takes to work. Suddenly, his cell phone buzzed, and he instinctively began to attend to a text message. His wife looked over at him in disbelief and asked, "What are you doing?" When Eric failed to respond, she escalated her concern and screamed, "What are you doing!"

Eric looked at his distraught wife and realized that he was not mentally present in the car with his family. Instead, he was on his way to work, doing what he did every morning: combining the tasks of communicating and driving to remain ahead of his steady workload. However, in the moment, he was unaware that he was jeopardizing the safety of his two sons, sleeping in their car seats, as well as himself and his wife. Before this incident, the inherent danger in sending a text message while driving had never occurred to him. Today, texting while driving is illegal in some states. But that doesn't seem to stop the Erics of this world.

Eric's story is symptomatic of many executives who lose touch with what is important when trying to do more than they can handle. They fail to recognize not only the dangers, but also how much of life they are missing out on. Eric is an example of a person who is "chasing" to get it all done at any cost.

When it comes to managing your life, what's your story? Can you relate to Elizabeth, Phil, and Eric? Whatever your personal experience, regardless of how overwhelmed you feel, you can rest assured that you are not alone. Many of us are longing for more time for ourselves and looking for a way to manage time so that we are getting things done and living more life.

TIME SHORTAGE

Ask anyone what they want more of and time is sure to be at the top of the list (or at least a close second to money and sleep). We live with the persistent thought that there just isn't enough time. So where did all of the time go? With modern advances in technology one would think that we would experience more time to do what we want to do, but that's not the case. We've run into a wall regarding our current thinking about productivity and effectiveness. Our old models are obsolete and ineffectual. The to-do list no longer works; neither do weekly objectives. We are far beyond the scope of what those practices were designed to do. There are valid reasons why we find ourselves operating in a state of wanting more time. We'll illustrate how these factors have been creeping steadily into our lives to make our current productivity practices insufficient for the life and work demands of the twenty-first century. Understanding why feeling overwhelmed has become a common condition in today's world and why it is important to develop a new relationship with time is the first step in learning new practices and gaining more control of your life.

Pace

We live in a new and unprecedented time. Life around us moves faster and at previously unthinkable speeds. Just look at the popular television show *Extreme Makeover: Home Edition*. The producers identify a family in need of a new home, and then a crew of contractors, designers, and volunteers swoops in, tears down the old house, pours the expanded foundation, puts up a new frame, paints and furnishes the new house, and landscapes the property. In one week, while the family enjoys a Disney vacation, the crew builds a beautiful new home and then the family moves back in.

Books are printed and shipped overnight. With e-mail, documents are transported instantaneously. News events are broadcast as they happen. Vacation photographs and videos are sent instantly by phone. When you stop and think about the world that existed only twenty-five or thirty years ago, it seems as though everything back then happened in slow motion.

If you were working in a typical office during the 1970s or even in the 1980s, you might remember having an inbox sitting on your desk. It was a physical, oblong box, often labeled "IN." Stacked on top of it, or on the other side of the desk, sat the box labeled "OUT." During the day, people made requests directly: They used telephone calls, mail (of the "snail" variety), interoffice memos (physically copied and distributed), and for companies doing business internationally, telex messages. There was no videoconferencing, no e-mail, and no instant messages. By the end of the day, almost all work tasks were completed; the inbox was empty and even the documents were filed away. While there were exceptions, this was the way most people worked.

Magnitude

The volume of what we deal with each day is also unprecedented. There are many new ways to be bombarded by advertising, information, and opportunities on our music devices, cell phones, smartphones, and computers. Sophisticated picture-in-picture technologies on TV and computer screens make it easier to watch multiple shows at one time, and with digital recording devices, we won't miss anything.

We once relied on a set of hardcopy encyclopedias to look up information on a subject; now, Internet search engines allow us to access resources instantaneously. Digital cameras make it possible for people to take hundreds of pictures, creating a quagmire of photo files embedded in the hard drives of their computers. Just a decade ago, most families took only a few family pictures each year.

The dramatic change in the cost of computer storage has now made mass storage affordable. However, the by-product of cost-effective memory is that, because it is available, we fill it with more information.

Clutter

It's not only the glut of information, but also the physical clutter that bombards us. We consume and accumulate more things and new technological toys, but we don't make choices about what we already have. For example, we have clothes for different seasons, activities, and sizes. We have closets full of clothes, yet we might complain about having nothing to wear for a given occasion. We have books, old magazines, and dated reports we don't throw out. We might have a garage or basement full of older-model televisions, computer monitors, and DVDs we don't watch anymore, and outdated technologies such as VCRs and cassette tapes.

The clutter includes the e-mails in our inboxes, electronic files in desktop folders, and the papers in our file cabinets or on our desks. There is so much to do because so much fills our space as we accumulate projects, materials, and goods we don't use.

Could this situation account for the emerging field of professional organizers, the popularity of *feng shui* to help us create harmonious space, and workshops that instruct us to clean out closets, empty our kitchen junk drawers, and eliminate expired, worn-out products from our medicine cabinets?

Complexity

We live in a 24/7 world that offers both convenience and complexity. Globalization means we now deal across continents, time zones, and cultures. Many of us no longer have standard office hours, as employees around the world need to collaborate in virtual teams. Sections of this book were written virtually via an Internet phone connection, with one person in China and another in New England.

We have a myriad of different technologies for communicating with one another across distances and time zones. Computers have become more than data-entry machines. Equipped with microphones, video cameras, and color printers, computers are multipurpose publishers, televisions, radios, telephones, scanners, and fax machines.

We have integrated many kinds of media into everything we do. Not too long ago, writing a report, giving a talk, or holding a meeting or conference call were separate tasks. Now, meeting presentations include slides with video and audio clips, and you can host a web meeting so that people can, from remote locations, ask you questions while you talk. You can e-mail or print full-color handouts. Everything has become flashier, more integrated, and more complex.

The increase in volume and speed of access to information adds to the complexity of managing it all. We have much more data available to us and we have easy access to it; the challenge is making sense of it, learning from it, and synthesizing it fast enough. A decision you made yesterday may change tomorrow because of new data.

The increase in volume and speed of access has also increased the complexity of our lives. Think about it: A person can contact you at your home phone (if you still have one) or by cell phone, office phone, e-mail at home, e-mail at work, instant message, text message, fax, U.S. Postal Service, overnight mail, and/or courier service. On a daily basis, you may carry a cell phone/smartphone on your belt or in your purse, wear a Bluetooth receiver in your ear, and pack a laptop in your briefcase or backpack. You may think that with all of this "productivity firepower" we would be producing at a higher level and with greater ease. But here's the reality: We're not. E-mail is the perfect example.

E-Mail Invasion

Instead of being a solution for efficient communications, e-mail inundates and controls us. Researchers at the Radicati Group estimated that the number of e-mails sent worldwide per day in 2009 was approximately 247 billion. By 2013, this figure will more than double to 507 billion. About 81 percent of all e-mail traffic is spam. In 2009, around 1.4 billion people sent non-spam e-mails. That number is expected to increase to 1.9 billion in 2013.

Advertising and e-mail have a lot of similarities, yet we deal with them quite differently. We see advertisements daily in magazines and on television, billboards, elevators, buses, and subways, but if the ad isn't for something that we are interested in, we discard or ignore it. We don't feel that the ads are directed at us personally. With e-mail, however, even when we are one of five million people receiving a message, because our name is included as an addressee, it can feel as if the e-mail is personal and we must open and read it.

Can you imagine if every time you watched television you had to categorize every commercial, think about its content, send it to other people, and then file it away? You'd go crazy. Yet that is what many of us do with our e-mail messages. Our inboxes are full of messages because we don't know what to do with them.

THE LOST ART OF BEING EFFECTIVE

There is a difference between being effective and being productive. Productivity is a measure of how much you do with the resources you have in a given amount of time. Being productive means you are *producing* something.

You can be productive on a manufacturing line, or while writing a report, or by improving your sales results. Productivity can be a static number or quota.

Effectiveness, on the other hand, is like a muscle: something you can flex and build. *Effectiveness* is an ability; it is a measure of how you engage in a set of actions that produces the desired outcome. It is also a skill that has gone largely unexamined in terms of what we mean by being "effective in life." Being effective means that you choose what you focus on and where you place your efforts in order to cause an intentional effect on your life.

To be effective, you must first ask yourself, "What do I want to accomplish?" You cannot be effective without consciously choosing to be.

This book examines effectiveness as it relates to managing your minutes, hours, days, weeks, months, years, and life. We'll look at specific areas of our lives that cause stress and anxiety—for example, e-mail, clutter, the inability to choose priorities, and the lack of planning.

LEARNING TO CHOOSE

One of the muscles required to lead an effective life is choice. Choices that you resist making will persist. For instance, countless e-mails in your inbox are going to persist until you make some choices about them or until your system manager or company policies choose for you and cut you off from receiving or sending any more messages.

The holiday season gives us a good example of the difference between effectiveness and productivity. How many people do you know who complete all their shopping, send all their cards, spend weeks decorating their houses, and then find when the holidays are over, they are left wondering, "All that for this?" In the end the holidays are a huge letdown. These people were incredibly productive, yet all that productivity didn't result in a satisfying experience. Perhaps they were not especially effective at enjoying and relishing the holidays with family and friends.

What if, right now, you pulled out your calendar for October, November, and December and scheduled time for buying holiday cards, editing your list, and writing and mailing your cards? What if you scheduled time to make a list of everyone you were going to buy presents for? And, while you're at it, what if you scheduled time on three evenings and four weekend days to go holiday shopping? How would that change your experience of the holidays? What if you completed your shopping and shipping by the first of December, leaving you the whole month to enjoy the holidays, the parties, and extra time with your family? What would that experience be like?

Maybe you are already a careful planner for the holidays. What if you were able to plan new rituals such as a spa day or a ski trip to replenish yourself? Maybe you could visit a nursing home, a children's hospital, or a homeless shelter to spread some goodwill.

Being effective is not only about getting things done, but also about enjoying what is important to us. Our inability or unwillingness to schedule the time to plan major events in our lives, such as holidays, contributes to our harried schedules. Having insufficient time to get everything done leaves us with the experience of not feeling satisfied with life. It's the lack of choosing that contributes to our sense of being overwhelmed and stressed out, of falling behind, and any other terms we may use to describe not being in control of our lives.

Effectiveness is our key to experiencing a sense of accomplishment, pride, and peace. At the end of the day, ask yourself, "Did I operate in a way consistent with my vision, purpose, or goals in life? Did I make a difference?" Or are you left with the nagging notion of, "I didn't even start half of what I set out to do today. I left a mountain of work behind me. And, oh, I remembered something else that I promised to do but forgot." We need to set up our lives for effectiveness and structure our time so that we can have the life we want to live.

Effectiveness is at the core of living a satisfying life. You make choices from moment to moment; you set a compass to guide your life. Along the way, you may encounter rough seas and may have to correct or change your course to navigate through them. The core practices in this book will support you in being effective and productive and, more than anything, happy with the life that you're living. At the core of being effective is the ability to make choices.

Quantity vs. Quality

When my daughter was young, I, Rosemary, was a working single mom who was trying to somehow get it all done. I was always in a rush to get to work, to the store, and to school, and I felt caught up in a whirlwind that never stopped. When I picked my daughter up from child care, I was still winding down from work, rushing home to cook dinner and help her with homework, and then off to bed. One evening, as I kissed her good-night, I had an epiphany. I realized that I had snagged my daughter into my whirlwind and she was spinning as fast as I was. I knew that if I didn't do something to stop the swirl, we were going to miss out on sharing a whole part of our lives together.

I instituted what we called "us time"—a time with no other responsibilities or distractions, a time for us to converse each day. Picking her up from child care on my way home from work became our special time together. I turned off the radio as we drove so that we could talk, and she would tell me what was happening in her life. It was our way to reconnect and transition from business executive and student to Mom and Daughter. Obviously, that wasn't the only time we were alone together, but, that short time in the car was a wonderfully effective way to experience something truly important together. With just twenty-four hours in a day, having even a half hour dedicated to being "in the moment" with someone important to you can be the true definition of quality time.

We think of time as something that can be controlled or manipulated, and that, by doing so, we'll be able to accomplish all of our goals. In truth, we have much more to do than time to do it in. All the time management in the world cannot counteract the reality that there are only twenty-four hours in a day, of which about eight are usually designated for sleep.

The source of productivity isn't the quantity of things that you complete; it's completing the things that deliver the most quality in the ways that you measure quality. For instance, you could measure quality in terms of satisfaction or in terms of impact.

It is important to redefine what is important in terms of quality. It is easy to fool ourselves into thinking that as long as we are checking off items on our lists, we are doing all right. That's only half the story; the other half is about being mindful of what's truly important in our lives.

HOW EFFECTIVENESS DRAMATICALLY INCREASES PRODUCTIVITY

A natural outcome of being clear about what's important to you, and of consciously choosing what you are doing and setting yourself up to do it with all of your resources, is that you will be much more productive. The key to increasing your productivity (i.e., your output) is to work on your effectiveness.

Last March, a client sent us a bouquet of ten beautiful red and white tulips. When we got them, the directions said to cut off the ends and put them in fresh warm water. We followed the directions, and all day long we had a touch of spring in the office. The next day, we were out of the office and unable to water the flowers. When we returned, the tulips had all drooped down around the vase.

It was sad to see them wilted like that; they were so vibrant the day before and a welcome addition to the office. We took them out of the vase, clipped their ends again, and poured in fresh warm water. The next morning, the tulips were again standing up straight in their vase as though nothing had ever happened.

We like to think of that story in terms of effectiveness. Flowers are designed to bloom; all they need are the right conditions: water, nutrients, and sunlight. As human beings, we are designed to be effective and productive. What gets in our way is that we don't create the right conditions in our life to be effective and productive, and so we wilt, like a flower without enough water. Once we restore the conditions that optimize our effectiveness, we find our productivity in bloom again. You will learn in later chapters about the different kinds of support you can create for yourself to restore the conditions you need.

Acting in Your Own Best Interest

If you recognize yourself in the stories of Elizabeth, Phil, and Eric at the beginning of the chapter, and see the futility of what you are doing, that is an important step to doing what it takes to change your behavior. It is not enough to gain insights into how to structure your time differently. You also need to shift the way that you think about time.

Let's face it; the world isn't going to slow down anytime soon. People are still going to send you e-mail, expecting an instant response, as if you have nothing else in the world to do but stare at your screen, waiting for their message to come through so that you can read it and respond. You are still going to be invited to meetings where 1) the outcome of the meeting is unclear, 2) people wander in late and you restart again and again, 3) people respond to their e-mail and text messages while in the meeting, and 4) the moderator runs out of time and makes requests, pleas, and demands for follow-up actions in the last two minutes. You are still going to have an unreasonable amount of work heaped on you without anyone thinking through whether there is enough time to do it all.

There are some things that you can change and others that you have to work around. The process of choosing what you can and cannot change gives you the power to use your time, energy, and focus to accomplish what you deem is most important. It allows you to "have more time for you" and to take charge of your life.

THE DANCE BETWEEN EFFICIENCY AND EFFECTIVENESS

Sometimes you find yourself being extremely efficient at certain tasks during the day, but feeling quite ineffective by the end of the day.

And sometimes you feel that you've had a very effective afternoon, even when you know that the way you accomplished your tasks was anything but efficient. How can this be?

You say someone performs a task or job efficiently when they achieve the result in the least amount of time with the least amount of energy and resources. In sports, you hear about a runner using his energy efficiently or a baseball pitcher throwing efficiently. Again, these individuals are doing the job with the least amount of energy, time, and resources.

Effective behavior comes from being clear about what is most important to you and then acting on it to fulfill that vision, value, or concern. We say, "She is an effective teacher," or "This is an effective method for doing xyz." Effectiveness includes doing what you are doing because it serves your purpose or fulfills your objectives.

Here's an example you may recognize: How many times have you just "dashed off" an e-mail to respond to a colleague, just to get it done, only to find five e-mails later that if you had stopped and picked up the phone and discussed the issue, it would have been resolved much more satisfactorily and quickly?

When you are clear about what you want to accomplish and are able to balance your time and resources to meet your goals, you are in the dance of effectiveness and efficiency. The elements are:

- Clarity about the exact objective
- Finding the right balance between speed, quality, and resources (or price)

When a situation is unclear or less well defined, using the "efficiency muscle" doesn't work. When you head into action right away without a clear picture of where you are headed, you may be the most efficient person at crossing items off your to-do list and doing pointless tasks that are not on your purpose list. None of this gets you any closer to your goal.

This book presents efficient processes and methodologies that will support you in achieving your goals and that will help you be effective at accomplishing what you say is most important.

THE PROCESS OF LIFE IS TO GENERATE THINGS

In our productivity and effectiveness workshops, group participants are sometimes asked to make a list of everything they have to do. While they are writing, we'll offer some tasks to consider adding to their lists; for example, "Update your car registration, pay your bills, and schedule lunch with an old friend."

After five minutes everyone is told to stop writing and asked, "What are you experiencing?"

Rich, a new hire at a company said, "Ugh. There's so much to do, I can't even write it all down."

Marcie, a young mother and an up-and-coming executive said, "I haven't even scratched the surface yet. I've written only the things that need to be done at work." And everyone else chimed in with similar responses.

Asked if they wanted more time to write, everyone responded in unison, "Yes." When time was up five minutes later, Marcie commented, "The more time I take to write down the things that I need to do, the more anxious I get. The more anxious I get, the more I'm clear I don't have the time to get it all done. But I have to get it all done!"

And that is the dilemma.

Life is a generative process. As such, you will typically find you have more to do, not less.

Our minds work faster than our mouths, our hands, or our feet. We will always—yes, always—generate more things to do, more things to think about, more things to desire, and more and more. Research indicates that the average person talks to himself or herself about 50,000 times a day.[1] Generating more isn't the problem. Failing to make choices is. It's about choosing now, not later.

PRODUCTIVITY REQUIRES CONSTANT PRACTICE

You have already read why having too much to do is not your fault. Even so, you still have to deal with the reality of the tasks at hand. You didn't create the overload, but you need to find a way to bring order back to your life. We don't like that we have a hole in the ozone layer of our atmosphere, but it is a problem we need to fix nonetheless.

Productivity comes from your experience, knowledge, and expertise. If you were to poll our friends and family, they will tell you that we're not perfect. We may not always be prompt and may not respond to every e-mail or voice mail in a timely manner. And yet here we are, consulting, coaching, and training people in how to live effective lives. Even we wrestle with managing the pace, magnitude, and complexity of life. What is different, however, is that each of us is able to accomplish more of what's important to us than ever before because we continually practice what we've learned about productivity.

Being productive as well as effective is a lifelong journey. It's also a daily practice. You will never possess productivity. You need to continually renew it. After you eat, you don't stay full forever. You might have issues about what you eat, how much, or how little, but you know that eating is not something you do only once. You know that you have to eat every day to maintain your strength and keep your body nourished. The same is true with any practice in which you want to achieve mastery. Whether you are learning to meditate, play the piano, or clear your inbox, you need to do it consistently every day. You can't do it once and be done with it. That would be like saying, "I practiced the piano one time and now I can play like a maestro." In fact, being productive and effective takes daily practice.

Yet, despite all the evidence, most people still believe that they shouldn't have to practice to gain proficiency. Why? For one thing, people tend to confuse hearing something for the first time and actually learning it. You may hear advice about being more effective. You may agree with what you hear. But actually putting it into practice requires change—and it takes time.

In reality, we often need to relearn something over and over until it becomes a part of us. It's not enough to say, "I have this one insight and now I'm set." Now that you've had that insight, you need to transform it into an action that you can integrate into daily practice. Subsequent chapters will provide maintenance practices for you to use to live an effective life.

What does it take to become a master in effectiveness? In his book *Mastery*, George Leonard talks about the "mastery curve," whereby learning any new skill involves relatively brief spurts of progress, each of which is followed by a slight decline to a plateau somewhat higher than the previous level. "To take the master's journey," he says, "you have to practice diligently, striving to hone your skills, to attain new levels of competence."[2] And you have to be willing to spend most of your time on a plateau—to keep practicing even when you seem to be getting nowhere.

The other problem is thinking that we already know how to gain control. Many people think they already have the strategies and practices they need to succeed amid the speed and complexity of our lives. Then we blame ourselves for not managing ourselves well enough. We call these coping strategies. The next chapter explores these options and why they fail.

2

THREE COPING
STRATEGIES THAT
DON'T WORK

The challenge is in the moment, the time is always now.
                                          —*JAMES BALDWIN*

Because we are often human *doings,* rather than human *beings,* we've cleverly devised ways to keep ourselves on top of the great mountain of things to do. As much as these tactics seem to help in the moment, they only trick us into thinking we are doing something about the problem.

This chapter describes the three most common coping strategies: procrastinating, multitasking, and saying you're too busy. We explain why they fail and how eliminating them leads to greater satisfaction, less stress, improved productivity and more time for you.

STRATEGY 1: PROCRASTINATING

The dictionary definition of procrastination is to defer action; to put off until another day or time; to delay. A procrastinator is someone who postpones work (often out of laziness or habitual careless-ness). Procrastination can be the culprit that hangs up projects and puts people into emergency mode. When we wait until the last minute to get things done, it creates stress. When we identify ourselves as procrastinators, we become self-fulfilling prophecies or prisoners of our self-indictments. Why would we ever put that label on ourselves? For some people, procrastinator has become an acceptable label, and its allure captures us in the trap of procrastination.

The Allure

People under the allure of procrastination often say things like:

- "The feeling of wanting to do it hasn't hit me yet. Maybe I'll be in the mood later, so I'll wait."
- "So many more good things could come up right now. I want to keep my options open."
- "I can get that done later."
- "I can count on myself to complete work at the last minute, because it's the deadline that provides the discipline."

Part of the allure of procrastination is that it tricks you into thinking that things can actually happen later. The relief that you feel by procrastinating is in not having to commit to the task now. However, it is a temporary relief, not a solution.

As an example, your coworker is fretting and says to you, "We need to get this report done, but I don't have any time to squeeze it in." You say, "Let me handle it. I can do it later." Your coworker says, "Wonderful. Copy me when you finish it, okay?"

You haven't actually scheduled time to write the report. Instead, by putting it off until sometime later, you achieve the following results:

- You buy yourself time. If you simply tell someone that you will do something later, most of the time people won't press you as to when "later" is.
- You leave your coworker thinking, "Great. She said that she'll do it and that she'll copy me, so I don't have to worry about it."

Now both you and your coworker are freed up. You saved the day by saying that you would take on the task; your coworker thinks that you are a genius and gives you positive reinforcement for being on top of the game. You've been able to feed your habit for being the hero by being the one who came up with the resolution, and you didn't have to spend any time to do the task—at least not yet. Now you can look for more things to do and more ways to save the day while receiving more positive reinforcement for your actions.

The Stress Cost

Despite the temporary relief and sense of accomplishment you felt when offering to take on the report, there is also a cost to both you and your coworker. By putting off the task to write the report until later, you have ensured that you'll be adding stress to your life and maybe to your coworker's life, too. By not even checking whether you have the time, let alone scheduling the time, you are building up tension around if, when, and how you are going to do this task.

Also, when the deadline nears and you have to produce the report, you will most likely end up delaying some other deliverables that you promised to somebody else, thereby adding more tension and stress to follow through on your current tasks. It's like a snowball, and it takes up psychic energy and psychic space for something that you know you need to do.

Here's another example of the cost of procrastination. It is the end of the year and you need to give your accountant year-end reports and receipts so that he can create your company's financials. The only thing holding him up is that you have not accounted for all of the expenses that offset the revenue you received to reduce your taxable income. It is exceedingly tedious to go through twelve months of expenses. You dread it and keep putting it off. You beat yourself up for not taking the one hour it might have taken each month to do the job right. And because you are so disappointed in yourself for being in this predicament, you put if off even longer.

This is not the kind of work that you enjoy doing, which is why you have put it off to begin with. Just the thought of finances, taxes, and money makes you queasy. Your palms sweat at the idea of going back to last January and pulling out all those receipts. You build a case around how awful this task is; the bigger the case, the more you justify why you don't need to it right now. So you "awful-ize" the experience.

Only now you are in the position of not being able to delay any longer. Your accountant won't prepare your tax return if you don't have the information to him by the close of business today. You know that it will be nearly impossible to find another accountant who will take you on as a client at this late date. If you don't ac-count for your expenses today, Armageddon will come. You cannot procrastinate any longer. This is it.

You are drained emotionally by this process and having to spend time that you could have used on something productive to catch up on a task that you should have handled throughout the year.

No Time to Delegate

Another cost of procrastination is there's no time to delegate. If you had been more proactive in starting the task of gathering the year's receipts, you could have enlisted help. You could have hired a bookkeeper or a college student. Now you can't give the job to anybody.

You think, "If only I had blocked out time every month to do my finances, I would have been able to spread out this task through-out the entire year and my finances would be in beautiful shape. Everything would have been checked and double-checked, and there wouldn't have been any errors. Now I only have eight hours to do my finances. I will get them done; however, I won't have time to check for errors, and I will be stressed out for the entire day."

Getting things done at the last minute gives you the illusion of productivity, because you think that as long as you get the job done in the minimum amount of time, there is no other cost. You think that the job you are putting off isn't preying on your mind and that it isn't costing you anything. You don't like the rush, but you'll come through and do it once again. And, yes again, you'll come through at the cost of unnecessary stress, panic, and questionable results.

The Impact

One of the areas of my (Rosemary's) business that I resist is the record-keeping and accounting. I just don't want to do it. I dislike doing it. I find it to be too detail-oriented and tiresome for my taste. As long as I get the invoices out, checks cashed, credit cards processed, and the bills paid, life works, right?

The danger here is allowing the thinking that "I don't want to do it"—and therefore don't need to do it right now—run the show. It dulls the senses to the true cost and impact of procrastination. The temporary fix that we get from delaying a decision to take action will inevitably come back to haunt us. At some point the piper will need to get paid. This item will need to be paid attention to—and resisting it or delaying doesn't change the situation; it only prolongs the agony of not doing it. We all know this intellectually, but that doesn't seem to be sufficient to change our behavior. Taking stock of the true impact that procrastination has on us emotionally, physically, and energetically may help to create some momentum and action.

Consider this scenario: There is a pile of papers, receipts, invoices, and bills that need to be sorted and handled. You say to yourself, "I don't want to do it right now. I'll get to it later." And you turn your attention to something else. A few hours later, you look at the pile again, with disdain and disgust, and say, "I still don't want to do it," but this time you're beginning to feel the pangs of guilt and worry because you have a vague sense that some bills are due and deadlines are approaching. It's difficult to face this just now, and besides, you have a meeting in a few minutes, so you soothe yourself and say, "Tomorrow, for sure. I'll get to it." That night you wake up suddenly with the nagging thought that a payment to a vendor is due today and the invoice is in that pile! You resolve to tackle the pile of papers first thing in the morning.

The next day arrives and your morning goes awry when a customer calls with an urgent request. It is late afternoon when you receive an e-mail from your manager asking for one of the items in that pile that you've been procrastinating. Your stomach churns and you begin to turn your attention to the pile again. Now you're angry with yourself for delaying and begin screaming to yourself, "Why do I always put things off!" You're worried that your boss doesn't think you're keeping up. You pride yourself on paying bills on time; now your payment is late with a valued vendor and you're concerned about your reputation. You begin to doubt your own ability to stay ahead. You begin to justify in your mind that you had too many other things to do and just couldn't get to it any sooner. You begin to blame others for constantly adding things to your already full plate. You feel overwhelmed, frustrated, and disempowered (with a dollop of shame for good measure).

The impact of procrastination on our psyches and well being is immense. The impact shakes us at our core. We begin to doubt ourselves and feel guilty, shameful, and inadequate. The impact has a cumulative effect—every time we procrastinate on something, it deepens and reinforces our self-doubt and erodes our well being. This costs us in terms of our ability to be present in our lives, because when we're distracted by our self-berating, we aren't able to be our most resourceful and effective.

If you want to fulfill your purpose in life, then you need to handle your finances. It doesn't mean that *you* have to do them; it means that you have to have them *handled*.

Getting back to one's purpose—for example, why you are engaged in your business in the first place—helps you to see that when you don't maintain accurate information on your finances, you put a lid on your future and the contributions you are here to make. Purpose helps people shift the situation; it brings clarity. And in this example, clarity about how to handle finances will allow you to experience the following:

- Relief from knowing that your business finances are in order and there to support you.
- Calm from knowing what's real and what's not real, so you can plan, act, do, adjust, and take on new marketing opportunities.
- Peace of mind from knowing that because your finances are well managed, you can spend more time being creative (by contrast, not knowing your financial status can limit your creativity).
- Certainty in knowing what the score is, since you are the one playing this game of life.

Life is an important game, but it's still a game. And if you don't know what the score is, how can you ever know if you are winning?

Pay Now or Pay Later with Interest

Everyone, even the most efficient and effective person, has something they resist doing. We've all avoided a job by shipping it off to "Later Land." The question becomes how much do you pay for that resistance in the long run?

Procrastination is a way of trying to get out of having to pay the time for doing something. We all play the game thinking that "later" will never come and we will never have to pay the time to do the task. But there's no avoiding the reality that you'll have to pay the time at some point. Even if you delegate or pay someone else to do the job, you are still paying for it to happen. The question becomes: Do you want to pay now or do you want to pay later with interest and penalties?

We Deceive Ourselves

The scientific method is a systematic means of collecting and analyzing data objectively. Without some level of external objectivity, we are tempted to automatically look for data that supports our original assumptions or hypotheses. We are predisposed to look only for evidence that proves our perspectives and to reject information that doesn't verify our thinking. As Roger Bacon, a thirteenth-century philosopher and early developer of the scientific method, might have described it today, human beings are programmed to deceive themselves.

Because we are programmed to deceive ourselves, we find that procrastination is part of that self-deception. We deceive ourselves into thinking that we have more time later, and we don't.

The scientific method that we are proposing here is a way to have checks and balances so that you can be more objective; so that you can be the cause of how you live and choose how you use the time available in your life. Without those checks and balances, you will deceive yourself, by design.

Using Fear as the Culprit

When people procrastinate, it is often because they are afraid of doing a specific task, usually because they don't think they can do it or do it well, and because they are fearful of what other people might think. This underlying fear of failing is why we don't want to do the task and why we look for ways to avoid it altogether.

It's not a lack of confidence, although that may be part of the fear; it is usually something much broader than not feeling self-assured. Fear may be present when you make a commitment to do something and then avoid it at all costs. In those moments, people sometimes do things to numb themselves from the fear, like watching television. For others, it might be eating, exercising, or even housecleaning. What distraction keeps you numb to the fear?

Some people can't stand having something "hanging over their heads," and that engages them to act. The thought of not doing something to complete the task is torturous for them. They'll say, "It doesn't make sense to delay the inevitable; get it done and get it over with."

For many other people, though, the opposite is true. Then we find ourselves misusing time, not completing tasks when we say we will, and it often comes from being paralyzed by fear. You need to go to the doctor, but find that it's easier not to make that appointment because you are afraid the doctor will find something wrong. You put off writing to people on your holiday mailing list because you don't know what to say to them. Not wanting to sound trite, you just don't send the cards at all. These are examples of how the fear of failure becomes the accomplice to procrastination.

STRATEGY 2: THE MYTH OF MULTITASKING

We have been studying the multitasking phenomenon for many years, and we want to share this lesson with you: You may think you can do two or three different things using different senses at the same time, but experience tells us that you can't—not without a sharp drop in quality.

Every Saturday, we have a phone conference with a close group of friends and business associates. We have been meeting regularly for four years, and we help each another confront the self-limiting beliefs that we have about ourselves. It is an intimate group. This morning, our leader said, "I want everyone here to agree that you'll be 100 percent present during the call and not be making breakfast, checking e-mail, or doing something else for the next hour." Everyone in the group was very upset from that request. There was complaining, dissension, and outright refusal. No one could make the promise not to multitask during the phone call. We know the pitfalls of multitasking; we teach others to set up structures against it. Yet, in that moment, it was impossible to promise to be there "100 percent."

After forty-five minutes of group conversation, one of us said, "The best I can do is promise to keep this request in front of me during the call, and I'm going to ask that you, as our leader, restate the promise at the beginning of each call and mention it again a half hour into our call. And if I find myself drifting away, I'll come back. And that's the best I can do, because, even after all these years, I am still bitten by the bug of multitasking."

Multitasking is not mind-wandering, when you let your thoughts drift off while you are doing a task. Multitasking is the conscious act of engaging in another activity while you are doing what you first set out to do.

When I, Rosemary, was young, growing up as the oldest of seven children, my mother showed me that multitasking was the way to get things done. In fact, when my mother would see my dad come home from work and just do one thing and then another rather than everything at once, she would say things like "Wouldn't my life be nice if I could take on just one thing at a time?" So I learned that multitasking was not only useful but also an honorable thing to do. It was the way to meet everyone's needs.

When I entered the workforce in my early adulthood, I managed several companies by multitasking. I even hired people based on their ability to multitask. I had a scoring system, and I would not hire people who didn't score high at multitasking during their interview. At that point in my life, I still thought I could get it all done; after all, I was one of the best jugglers out there. I accomplished a lot. It was only when I began looking at what results are produced, and what is and isn't effective, that I began to see the cost of multitasking.

I have studied the perils of multitasking. I have even taught people about its hidden costs, and yet I am still bitten by the bug. I find that I have to sit on my hands during some phone calls so that I will not do something else. I am clear that multitasking takes away my focus. I am clear that I cannot give 100 percent of myself to more than one thing at a time. I am clear that, when I do give 100 percent of my attention while I'm listening and speaking with someone, we move things forward in a much more effective way. Even though I know this, I'll still find myself multitasking.

This is why I like to talk about multitasking as an addiction. I'm no longer the little girl helping my mother take care of everybody and do everything. I'm not even the young woman juggling two businesses and a school-age daughter. I am now someone who knows there is a cost. Even so, I am still inclined to multitask.

Degrees of Awareness

Let's say there are 100 degrees of awareness of multitasking. At first we have a 20 percent awareness of our habit of multitasking. Then, when we start to examine our habit a bit more, we gain another 20 percent awareness.

Later, we adopt some practices to manage our habit, and now we are up to about 60 percent awareness.

Now we say, "That's good enough. I have practices I can count on. I'm done with my habit." Yet we are never, ever done. Habits die hard! Our habits lie dormant, looking for ways to resurface. Habits often reside beneath the surface of our consciousness—and unless we remain vigilant and aware, they will sneak up on us and reclaim their place in our repertoire of behavior.

The Cost of Multitasking

With all the technology available to us today, and the amount of time that we spend working in the virtual world, it is critical to understand how strong the habit of multitasking is and how large the cost is.

Do you remember Eric's story at the beginning of the book? He's the insurance sales executive whose wife caught him responding to messages on his cell phone while he was driving on the expressway with his two children in the backseat. Eric admitted to writing e-mails while driving, endangering his own life and the lives of others on the road and in his car. After realizing the possible impact of his multitasking, he became an evangelist for correcting the behavior and said, "I do not want this to happen to the people who work for me. If I was that out of control with multitasking, it could happen to them, too."

Fifteen years ago I, Rosemary, had an experience that cost $3,500 in car repairs and showed me how costly multitasking and driving can be. I was on my way to work and traffic was very slow on my exit ramp. We were backed up, everything was stop and go, and I decided that this would be a great time to put on my lipstick. A flatbed truck was in front of me, and somehow while looking in the mirror and putting on my lipstick I managed to take my foot off of the brake pedal and my car gently rolled into the truck.

I was shocked at the amount of damage this created and at such a slow speed. It's easy to relate to the costs of multitasking when it comes to operating a car, but there are similar, if not greater, costs in so many other areas of our lives.

It is easy to see how dangerous multitasking can be when we are driving. Whether we are driving and answering e-mail, talking on the phone, eating, or trying to apply makeup, we are endangering ourselves and others by dividing our attention. But there are similar, if not greater, costs in so many other areas of our lives.

Multitasking as a Human Capacity

Your brain can process words much faster than you can speak them. The average person's speaking speed is approximately 165 words per minute, but our brains can process several times that number. This means that when we listen to the average person talk, our brains have the capacity to attend to other things.[1]

We also have an amazing capacity to perceive many things at once. Think about it: We can see, hear, smell, taste, and touch all at the same time.

There are parallels between our amazing capacity and the capacity of a computer. On your computer, you can have many different programs open at once. You can be sending and receiving e-mail, word processing, reading a spreadsheet, and browsing the Web at the same time. However, at some point, if you have too many applications open, you reach a maximum capacity and your computer crashes.

We, too, are wonderfully created to handle many different tasks at once. Our bodies are phenomenal in their ability to multitask. However, just as there are limits to how much oxygen we can have in our bloodstream before the oxygen reaches a dangerous level, there are limits to how much we can multitask before it overwhelms our capacity to be effective.

Multitasking is not always bad; in fact, there are times when it is positively beneficial. When left unexamined, however, multitasking has a cost. And before you know it, you could be in critical care because multitasking doesn't have any symptoms. You feel good because you and everyone around you can see that you are getting things done. People see multitasking as a sign of strength. It shows how talented we are. However, we often don't know when enough is enough.

Structures to Avoid Multitasking

Do you feel powerless over multitasking? Like being in a recovery program, where you find people to support you to break your addiction, you, too, may need a support structure to stay focused on (or "stay present to") who or what is in front of you.

For example, before a conference call with a client, give yourself five minutes to clear your mind and eliminate distractions. Clean off your desk and make sure there is nothing on the computer screen other than what you are doing with the client. Create and keep an expected outcome of the call in front of you so that you can stay focused. It takes muscle; it takes conscious effort.

Try telling yourself, "Nothing else is important right now. For the next hour, I can't do anything else anyway, so let me relax and enjoy this call." You want to be present to what you are going to accomplish on the call so that you can create that outcome with the client. Putting in these structures will allow you to be much more focused and in the moment, which helps avoid multitasking.

Discerning When and When Not to Multitask

In pursuit of being effective, it is important to discern when it does and doesn't make sense to multitask. By setting up a structure, you can make room for your habit by choosing when to multitask and when not to. Then, when there is blank space in your calendar, or when you are off somewhere on a walk, you can let your habit out of the box. It's baseball season again, and a wonderful opportunity for multitasking is watching the Red Sox on television. You can cook dinner and clean up, wash and fold laundry, because neither the Red Sox nor the laundry needs 100 percent of anyone's attention (although, if you've ever watched them leave a relief pitcher in too long in the eighth inning, you can't be sure about that).

Then there are times to say, "Okay, habit, you've had your time; I'm focused now." Once you have a structure in place that allows you to stay focused, then if you drift off, oops, you drifted off, but now at least you can get back on track again.

There are great benefits to multitasking. However, what we need to ask ourselves is when do the benefits outweigh the costs?

Multitasking per se is not bad. It can be an asset when doing things that don't require our full attention. But we need to discern when multitasking is appropriate and when it is not. Like yelling in a library, there are times when multitasking does not suit the situation. We've certainly seen what can happen if we try to multitask while driving.

When you see multitasking as a strength, you must choose

when to use that strength. That's all. There's no reason to vilify it. It is a matter of discerning when it is time to multitask.

STRATEGY 3: DON'T BLAME ME, I'M TOO BUSY

There is a collective empathy around being overwhelmed: I won't blame you for being too busy to meet your commitments if you don't blame me. You can't have two conversations in the same day without someone telling you how busy or how overwhelmed they are, or how much they have to do. It's the Overwhelm Epidemic, the overwhelm excuse.

The sense of having too much to do has crept upon us slowly. We are like the frog that sits placidly in a pot of boiling water because the temperature has increased too slowly to perceive the change. Similarly, having overcommitted lives has become an accepted condition for us.

Thirty years ago, if you complained about having too much to do, your coworkers would have said, "Well, why don't you manage things better?" Now, it's commonplace for people to one-up each other in terms of who has more to do. Being inundated is seen as the new normal. If you are not swamped, then you are perceived as being a slacker.

The word *overwhelmed* may have bad connotations to some people. "We're not overwhelmed. Not us. Not the smart ones. Not the dedicated ones. We can power through it."

But sometimes you say, "Of course I can't do it. I have too much to do." The good news is that we are able to acknowledge that there is always going to be too much to do. The bad news is that we use it as an excuse to not do the things that we want to do, like to do, or need to do.

We need new practices and habits that will make us effective in this world with its increased pace, volume, and complexity. There is a phenomenon called an *inattentional blindness,* which is the inability to see what is right in front of us.[2] In this case, it is the inability to see what is causing us to be ineffective. In the next chapter, you will see why and what to do about it.

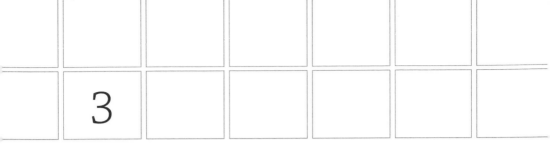

3

TIME AND YOU

Reality is merely an illusion, albeit a very persistent one.
—ALBERT EINSTEIN

"Put your hand on a hot stove for a minute, and it seems like an hour," Einstein said. "Sit with a pretty girl for an hour, and it seems like a minute. That's relativity."[1] A common experience that demonstrates the relativity of time is how the older you get, the faster time seems to pass. For children, summer seems to last a whole year long, which is a child's way of describing that summer went on forever. By the time you're in high school, it seemed like summer lasted two weeks. If you talk with people in their seventies and eighties, they will tell you that the three months of summer feel like a few days in their lives.

HOW PEOPLE EXPERIENCE TIME DIFFERENTLY

To illustrate the relativity of time, let's meet Fred and Amy.

Fred wakes up every morning at 5:30 a.m. He sets an alarm clock each night, even though he wakes up each morning before it goes off. He promptly gets out of bed, puts on his running gear and shoes (which he has laid out the night before), and goes outside to start his thirty-minute run. When he returns, he heads for the shower, shaves, dresses (he has laid out his suit, tie, socks, and shoes the night before), makes a protein shake (he has cut the fruit for the shake the night before), and drinks it while thumbing through the *Wall Street Journal*. At precisely 6:45 a.m., he is in his car heading to the office.

Amy wakes up every morning at 5:30 a.m. and curses the alarm clock as she slams the snooze button a minimum of three times. At last, she leaps out of bed when she realizes that she is in danger of missing an important client meeting. Like a bullet train, she dashes downstairs to put the laundry that she washed last night into the dryer so that she'll have clean socks to wear today. Then she runs to the bathroom, turns on the shower, and, as the water runs and gets hot, flies downstairs to turn on the computer before leaping back up the stairs to the bathroom and into the shower.

After the shower, while curling her hair, Amy listens to voice mail messages on her cell phone. She runs to her closet to dress, only to change clothes twice because the first jacket she put on had a stain on the lapel and the pants she planned to wear had a button missing. Then she races down to the laundry room to retrieve the clean socks from the dryer. Moving to her computer, she quickly glances at her e-mail to see if any important messages arrived overnight before she turns it off. Then she dashes to the kitchen to drink a glass of orange juice and is out the door driving to the train station. After a full-out sprint in her high heels, she catches the 6:45 a.m. train. This makes up a bit for the morning workout she missed.

Although Fred and Amy completed their morning routines in the same amount of time, their experiences of time were different.

Fred: Mr. On-Time

Now some of you may be thinking, "Look at how much more efficient Fred is. His morning routine is organized and, as a result, it seemed much less harried and stressed. And he was able to get in his workout, too." Sounds good. However, if this is Fred's only relationship to time, if he is always on time, if that is his first and only organizing principle, then he may have difficulty responding to changes or being flexible when the unexpected arises. However, we can all see how reliable he is, what a great trait that is, and how well he can be perceived on a team.

Amy: Ms. Make It All Happen

Then there's Amy. Some of you are likely thinking, "Slow down, girl. The world won't stop if you take two minutes and eat a bowl of cereal." However, when you are pushed up against a deadline, when your clients say they "have to have that data tonight or else," who would you rather count on? If you turn to Fred, he may say, "It's not in my schedule; you'll need to find someone else," or, "I can do it, but not until Friday." Amy, however, will move, shift, juggle, and come through for your client one more time.

How Amy views an hour is utterly different from how Fred views the same hour. One is not right or wrong or better than the other. However, allowing ourselves to think that everyone else thinks about time the way we do is a setup for disaster.

I'M IN THE ZONE

Do you know what it's like to get into a zone and lose all sense of time? It is a great place to be because it lets you accomplish a great deal of work. On the other hand, you can become so focused on something that you may overlook other commitments and deliverables you promised and even neglect your well-being. You don't stop to sleep or eat properly, the justification being that you are doing something that is as important. Your response to the situation is, "Do what you have to do to get it done at all costs!" When you reach this point, it is useful to schedule sufficient amounts of time in your calendar to complete the work and to set alarms to remind yourself when to start and stop working.

If you need to be up and running by 6:30 a.m., then set the alarm for 6:00 a.m. and give yourself thirty minutes to transition from a sleeping state to a waking state (most people cannot stop on a dime, and cannot start on one, either). If, once in motion, you're a whirlwind, then you'll need time to power down. So set reminders for yourself. If you need to leave for a meeting at 2:00 p.m., set an alarm to power down from what you're working on a half hour beforehand, so that you can come to a complete stop at two and head out to the meeting.

We recommend that people learn not to fight these tendencies, but to work with them. Realize there isn't anything "wrong" with the way you are, but you'll need to make allowances and accommodations to enhance your effectiveness.

RECOGNIZING DIFFERENT BEHAVIORS ABOUT TIME

Edward T. Hall, an anthropologist who studied societies and cultures, wrote *The Silent Language*, which is about the two distinct ways in which people experience time: monochronic and polychronic.[2]

Monochronic Behaviors

Hall wrote that monochrones see time as fixed, rigid, and absolute. They do one thing at a time. They view time commitments as critical. They are committed to jobs and projects. They are task-oriented. They adhere to plans, emphasize promptness always, and can be transactional in how they look at completing projects. Fred, "Mr. On-Time" from our earlier example, practices monochronic behaviors.

Monochronic behaviors are huge strengths. Without that devotion to production, planes and trains would neither depart nor arrive on time, assembly lines would be spectacularly unproductive, and many other task-time-based events would be impossible.

Polychronic Behaviors

Hall observed that polychrones perceive time quite differently. They see time as flexible. For a polychrone, a moment is capable of holding many events simultaneously. So they tend to do many things at once. They view deadlines as objectives rather than commitments. They are highly distractible, too. Polychrones are committed to people and relationships more than they are to time-related obligations. They are more inclined than monochrones to change their plans based on the significance of a relationship. Amy, "Ms. Make It All Happen" from our earlier example, practices polychronic behaviors.

Increasing Our Range of Motion

Have you ever awakened from a night's sleep to find that your neck is sore and that you have a limited range of motion when attempting to move your head from side to side? Our preferences for practicing monochronic or polychronic behaviors can also restrict our range of motion inside of that experience of time.

You have an opportunity to expand your range. And why shouldn't you? The wider your range, the more you can select options that fit the circumstances. Now you're not responding only one way—the way your natural tendency is. Instead you are more flexible and agile. Overall, you are more effective.

People governed by polychronic behaviors, who are more focused on relationships and the achievements that people make in project work, sometimes tend to feel intimidated by people who are deadline- and results-driven. Often, polychrones sit in judgment of monochrones, and vice versa. Polychrones hear, "You're not committed," or "You're not reliable." And monochrones hear, "You are more committed to getting the task done than you are to getting it done right," or "You miss opportunities to look at how things are changing around you, irrespective of your deadlines."

These judgments do no one any good. They thwart the true power of what can happen when both perceptions are accepted and practiced.

Overcoming Our Different Time Perspectives

The Ladder of Inference is a model developed by Chris Argyris[3] that describes the process by which we make conclusions. The climb up the ladder starts with data: Something happens. Based on the data, the event(s) that happened, we assign meaning. Based on that meaning, we make assumptions. Based on those assumptions, we draw conclusions. Based on those conclusions, we form beliefs. Based on those beliefs, we take action or inaction. Then we look only for data going forward that supports the conclusions that we have made.

In this example, we start out with the raw data, as if we had a video camera impartially recording the events as they happen. At 9:00 a.m., we see seven people in a meeting room sitting around a table. At 9:15 a.m., we see Leslie walk through the door and join the other people at the table. Our next step is to sort through the raw data and select what to pay attention to, and then to start an analysis of the event. Here is the step-by-step analytical process most people will follow:

• Focus on the fact that Leslie arrived fifteen minutes after everyone else.

• Assign meaning to this selected data. We say, "Leslie's late!"

• Make assumptions about Leslie being late. We say, "She thinks that her time is more valuable than ours."

• Draw conclusions based on our assumptions. "Leslie isn't committed to this project. We can't trust her to do her part to get the job done."

• Form beliefs based on our conclusions. "Leslie is not a team player. I mean, if she can't even do the basics of showing up on time, how can we ever depend on her around the big commitments?"

• Take action based on our beliefs. "We need to either micromanage Leslie or get her off the team. We definitely cannot give her something that needs to be done by a certain time."

• Filter out any data that runs contrary to our belief that Leslie does not respect other people's time. We will not notice the next ten meetings where she arrives at 9:00 a.m. sharp. We will only pay attention when she shows up late.

If we go back to the raw data of what happened, all we can say for certain is that seven people gathered around a table at 9:00 and one person arrived at 9:15. That's it. But we made it mean something else: "Leslie isn't committed; you can't trust her; she's not reliable; she's not a team member; and we're not going to assign her work."

Now, if we said to Leslie, "We agreed to meet at nine and you arrived at 9:15. What happened?" and she said, "Oh, my car broke down on my way to the train station and I had to get it towed," we might assign an entirely different meaning to Leslie's lateness, which would change the nature of our interaction.

As human beings, we cannot help but take trips up the Ladder of Inference. What we can do is notice when we have climbed the ladder and confused our assumptions for truth. Whenever we use the verb "is" to define a person's actions—"Leslie *is* late; she *is not* taking this meeting seriously"—we have made an assumption about a specific set of data. There isn't necessarily anything wrong with making this assumption; however, it may be that the assumption we made is far from accurate about the actual situation.

It's easy to draw an unfavorable conclusion about people who have time preferences that are different from our own. But doing so can impede our effectiveness. To be effective and productive, both personally and organizationally, we need to embrace the contributions offered by *both* polychronic and monochronic time orientations.

TIME SIGNATURES

Once, during a radio interview, the highly acclaimed British soul-pop singer Seal described how he creates music. "I like to use different types of time signatures when I write," he said.

On a sheet of music, a time signature consists of a pair of numbers (such as "4/4," but written one number over the other without a fraction line) that appears near the beginning of a musical staff (the five horizontal lines). It is one of the first things you see when you read music, immediately preceding the notes to play. You have to know what the time signature is to determine how many beats are in each measure so that you can play the piece. The time signature tells you how much "musical" time is in each frame.

It's a lovely way to think about time. Our lives have only so many measures. How do we wish to fill them? What do we want the beat to be?

It isn't too far a leap for us to think about the time in our lives, and that each measure of music represents a season of our lifetime. We need to consider what we want to accomplish. What do we want to create?

Being productive does not necessarily mean you are getting more done, but you are accomplishing what you want in your life, knowing that you are the composer. You get to decide the pace, the rhythm, and the time signature for your life's song. If you don't make those decisions, the music will never be created. The bottom line is you get to write and perform the song you want playing in your life. In Part Two, we'll take you through a step-by-step process of articulating what is important in your life and identifying what you want to spend more time doing.

PART
TWO

KNOWING WHAT YOU WANT

The life that conquers is the life that moves with a steady resolution and persistence toward a predetermined goal. Those who succeed are those who have thoroughly learned the immense importance of plan in life, and the tragic brevity of time.

—W. J. DAVISON

4

BEING CLEAR ABOUT WHAT IS IMPORTANT

If a man knows not what harbor he seeks, any wind is the right wind.

—*SENECA*

What will you do with your allocation of time on this planet? Who will you become? What will you have? What will you leave behind? When you know the answers to these questions, you will have clarity about what you want to accomplish with your life. Knowing these answers will give rise to what will enrich and enliven your life. It allows you to experience satisfaction, joy, and contentment with your life because it aligns with your own personal compass. When you have clarity, then all of a sudden you are in the driver's seat with your hands on the steering wheel and your foot on the gas pedal.

Being clear about what you are up to in life and where you are headed lets you set your internal GPS. Now you'll know your next steps. What's more, choosing what *not* to do will be much simpler.

Being unclear about what is most important in your life can lead to winding roads, detours, and bridges that may or may not take you to your destination. (Now, that might be fine for some people—maybe that's what they want from life.) The potential danger in not having clarity about what you want to do with your life is that it leaves you wide open to handling other people's issues and concerns, other people's desires, other people's emergencies . . . without ever getting to your own life.

In this chapter we invite you to engage in the following inquiry:

- What do you want?
- What is *most* important to you?
- What is the difference you want to make?

The answers to these questions will illuminate your path.

DETERMINING WHAT IS IMPORTANT

One of the keys to being productive, effective, and gloriously satisfied with your life is to get crystal clear about what is important to you, what matters the most to you, and why. When you are clear about what's important, you will find yourself engaging in purposeful actions to create and accomplish what you intend in life. Sometimes we are not wholly aware of what's most important to us. You can begin to gain greater clarity by considering your answers to the following questions:

- What do you long for?
- What do you strive for?
- Who do you look up to?
- What would you choose to do if you had limited time and resources?
- What do you consider to be the most important future contribution that you'll make?
- What do you give more than ordinary consideration or notice to?
- What has a considerable influence on your life?
- What holds a prominent place in your life?
- What comes forward when you contemplate these questions: What do you see as having the most meaning in your life? What do you care about most? What is most sacred to you?

Your responses to these questions will help get you in touch with what is truly important in your life. Consider that most of us don't know what is *truly* important to us. We know what we think should be important—rarely, though, have we boldly explored what, without question, is of utmost importance in our lives.

What matters to you? What is essentially true to and for you? I'm not talking about fleshly desires or worldly goods, but what naturally drives, motivates, fuels, arouses, calls, excites, interests, and satisfies you. What are you curious about? What brings you joy, ease, and laughter? Given all the things that you could do, what attracts you most? What do you find yourself thinking or talking about, even advocating for?

We've created a series of exercises to help you contemplate and clarify what is important to you.

Exercise: What Really Matters?

If you had more time, what would you do with it? What would you have that you currently do not have? Who would you be?

To use this exercise, you'll need a few sheets of paper, pen, and a timer, alarm clock, or stopwatch. The questions are designed to identify 1) what you consider the juice of life and 2) what you want more out of in life. Have fun with the questions, be playful and spontaneous, go with what comes to mind first, and see what emerges.

Question 1

Let's say that you had all the time (and resources) in the world to do whatever you wanted. What would you do? (Go crazy here; write down whatever comes to mind. Set your timer for two minutes and challenge yourself to write for the entire time without going back and editing. Go for quantity; the more items you can list, the better.)

Question 2

Take a look at what you've written in answer to question 1. Next, identify your favorite items from the list you've made.

Which things are the most fun, bring the most joy, create the most satisfaction or reward, and bring the most pleasure? Which items enliven you and call to you? Select the items that you want to spend more time doing. See if you can narrow the list down to between ten and fifteen items.

Question 3

Take a look at what you've written in answer to question 2. If you spent more of your life doing more of the things you have on your list, then how would you be experiencing life? How would you be feeling? Check all that apply in the Feelings Inventory shown in table 4-1.

Question 4

Take a look at the items you've checked off in table 4-1. It is a list of the feelings you experience while you are engaging in the activities listed in question 2 that bring you the most satisfaction, reward, and pleasure. Now, what needs are being met when you engage in these activities and experience these accompanying feelings? For example, if you feel appreciative, happy, and satisfied as a result of doing garden work, then you may be meeting your needs for beauty, self-expression, and challenge. Revisit your responses to question 2 and review your Feelings Inventory (table 4-1) again, and check all the fulfilled needs that apply in the Needs Inventory shown in table 4-2.

We intrinsically value the activities that meet our needs. Our behavior is guided by our drive to fulfill needs. Consider that everything on your calendar is there because it fills a need that you have. Consciously or unconsciously, we seek every avenue to meet our needs. When our needs are met, we are energized and likely to experience the feelings described in the Feeling Inventory table. When our needs are not met, then we are drained of energy and suffer distraction and distress.

Question 5

Our guess is that you want more time to experience the emotions you selected in the Feelings Inventory. These feelings are

Table 4-1. Feelings inventory.

FEELINGS INVENTORY		
☐ Absorbed	☐ Enthusiastic	☐ Passionate
☐ Adventurous	☐ Empowered	☐ Peaceful
☐ Affectionate	☐ Enthralled	☐ Perky
☐ Alert	☐ Excited	☐ Pleasant
☐ Alive	☐ Exhilarated	☐ Pleased
☐ Amazed	☐ Expansive	☐ Proud
☐ Amused	☐ Exuberant	☐ Quiet
☐ Animated	☐ Fascinated	☐ Radiant
☐ Appreciative	☐ Fulfilled	☐ Rapturous
☐ Aroused	☐ Free	☐ Refreshed
☐ Astonished	☐ Friendly	☐ Rejuvenated
☐ Awed	☐ Glad	☐ Relaxed
☐ Blissful	☐ Gleeful	☐ Relieved
☐ Breathless	☐ Glorious	☐ Safe
☐ Buoyant	☐ Glowing	☐ Satisfied
☐ Calm	☐ Good-humored	☐ Secure
☐ Carefree	☐ Grateful	☐ Sensitive
☐ Centered	☐ Gratified	☐ Serene
☐ Cheerful	☐ Happy	☐ Spellbound
☐ Clearheaded	☐ Helpful	☐ Splendid
☐ Comfortable	☐ Hopeful	☐ Still
☐ Complacent	☐ Inquisitive	☐ Stimulated
☐ Composed	☐ Inspired	☐ Surprised
☐ Confident	☐ Interested	☐ Sympathetic
☐ Compassionate	☐ Intrigued	☐ Tender
☐ Contented	☐ Invigorated	☐ Thankful
☐ Cool	☐ Involved	☐ Thrilled
☐ Dazzled	☐ Joyous, Joyful	☐ Tickled
☐ Delighted	☐ Jubilant	☐ Touched
☐ Eager	☐ Lively	☐ Tranquil
☐ Elated	☐ Loving	☐ Trusting
☐ Ecstatic	☐ Mellow	☐ Upbeat
☐ Effervescent	☐ Merry	☐ Vibrant
☐ Enchanted	☐ Moved	☐ Warm
☐ Encouraged	☐ Openhearted	☐ Wide-awake
☐ Energetic	☐ Optimistic	☐ Wonder
☐ Engrossed	☐ Overjoyed	☐ Wonderful
☐ Enlivened	☐ Overwhelmed	☐ Zestful

Source: Marshall Rosenberg, *Nonviolent Communication: A Language of Life* (Encinitas, CA: PuddleDancer Press, 2003), 212.

the by-product of having had your needs met. Review the Needs Inventory once more and identify five to ten of the needs that resonate with you the most. Then review the Feelings Inventory and identify the feelings associated with fulfilling the

Table 4-2. Needs inventory.

NEEDS INVENTORY		
☐ Acceptance	☐ Effectiveness	☐ Order
☐ Accomplishment	☐ Emotional safety	☐ Participation
☐ Affection	☐ Empathy	☐ Peace
☐ Appreciation	☐ Equality	☐ Purpose
☐ Authenticity	☐ Food	☐ Reassurance
☐ Awareness	☐ Freedom	☐ Respect
☐ Beauty	☐ Fun	☐ Rest/Sleep
☐ Belonging	☐ Growth	☐ Safety
☐ Celebration	☐ Harmony	☐ Security
☐ Challenge	☐ Honesty	☐ Self-expression
☐ Choice	☐ Hope	☐ Self-worth
☐ Clarity	☐ Humor	☐ Sexual expression
☐ Closeness	☐ Inclusion	☐ Shelter
☐ Cooperation	☐ Independence	☐ Space
☐ Communication	☐ Integrity	☐ Spontaneity
☐ Community	☐ Inspiration	☐ Stability
☐ Companionship	☐ Intimacy	☐ Stimulation
☐ Competence	☐ Joy	☐ Support
☐ Consciousness	☐ Laughter	☐ To be known
☐ Consideration	☐ Learning	☐ To be seen
☐ Consistency	☐ Love	☐ To be understood
☐ Contribution	☐ Meaning	☐ Touch
☐ Creativity	☐ Mourning	☐ Trust
☐ Discover	☐ Movement/Exercise	☐ Understanding
☐ Ease	☐ Mutuality	☐ Warmth
☐ Efficacy	☐ Nurturing	

Source: Marshall Rosenberg, *Nonviolent Communication: A Language of Life* (Encinitas, CA: PuddleDancer Press, 2003), 212.

need. An example is given in table 4-3. Last, identify the activities that most generate those feelings for you. The last column in table 4-3 is where the "more" in *more time for you* resides. These activities give you the best bang for your buck, the greatest payoff for your investment in time. These are the activities that really matter and are the most important for living a meaningful and rewarding life. You have just identified the ingredients you need for a life well lived!

Doing What Is Important
You should begin to see, as you make the lists described in this exercise, that what you do is almost always a function of what

Table 4-3. Associating needs and feelings with activities.

NEEDS THAT RESONATE THE MOST	WHAT THE NEED MEANS TO ME	FEELING ASSOCIATED WITH FULFILLING THE NEED	ACTIVITIES THAT GENERATE THE FEELING
Contribution	Being able to make a difference	Happy, Satisfied, Fulfilled, Grateful	Spending leisurely afternoons with my family Giving "More Time for You" presentations Volunteering at the food pantry

is important to you. Once you are clear about what is important to you, then you will be able to determine what you want to accomplish.

Living a life that matters means living a life that matters to *you*. You decide what is meaningful, significant, and paramount in your life. You draw the lines and color them in—and the clearer you are on what matters, the more effective you become at clearing the emotional, psychological, and physical clutter from your life.

Take a look in the mirror and ask yourself, What is the matter (the core) of my life that truly matters? Next, ask yourself, loudly this time, *What do I do about it?* To help you answer this question, read what authors Heike Bruch and Sumantra Ghoshal observed after a long study of the behaviors of managers in large multinational corporations: "Effective action relies on a combination of two traits: focus—the ability to zero in on a goal and see the task through to completion—and energy—the vigor that comes from intense personal commitment. Focus without energy devolves into listless execution or leads to burnout. Energy without focus dissipates into aimless busyness or wasteful failures."[1]

When you are in a state of knowing what is important and acting on it, you will be effective at executing purposeful action and operating with focus, vitality, and peace of mind.

When you are in the creative act of engaging in work or activities that are important to you, it produces the side effect of bringing out the best in you, of being the best of who you are. When you are engaged in what's important to you, you are being yourself in the deepest possible way.

Our motto is: Create your life and design your days. Creating your life begins with being clear about what you are up to and what you are out to fulfill in life. Establishing this, you can then work on being effective at living the life you create. You are clear about what's important, you've looked at what you want to accomplish, and you've created your life to carry it out. We're not interested in productivity for productivity's sake. Also, without being clear about what you are out to accomplish, you often have a sense of being forced, stressed, and over-whelmed by the tasks before you.

The following chapters will teach you techniques that allow you to get more done; however, the added benefit offers little relief unless you are clear about what's most important to you. So complete the exercise in this chapter first. If you want to be effective at living the life you create, you must first be clear about what you intend to accomplish in life and where you're headed. Then you can set yourself up to win. But if you don't know what you are up to or what's important, you might be productive, but not necessarily effective. That is, you'll get a great deal of work done, but the question remains: Will you have been effective at living a satisfying, rewarding, and meaningful life? Here are two examples that illustrate why it helps to be clear about what's important.

Rob Loves Pottery

A company that Rosemary co-founded hired young, talented people right out of college to sell computer equipment over the telephone directly to the purchasing and information technology departments of major corporations, and many of these new hires had never held a full-time job before. The company was very successful, doubling the number of employees year after year for five years.

There was a standard profile of the person that could jump in and do the job well: someone who loves to be on the phone, enjoys influencing others, or has any of the other characteristics that you would think a person needs to be successful in the sales role. However, there were some particularly successful people, such as Rob, who did not fit this profile.

New recruits received sales training, and, as part of the program, the trainer would say, "I want to know what's most important in your life. I want to know where you want to be ten years from now, twenty years from now. What do you want?"

Two-thirds of the group answered in dollars and cents, citing the money they wanted to make, the house they wanted to buy, and so on. Rob, who was one of the top (and youngest) producers, instead said, "When I came here, the talk of money didn't mean anything to me, but I liked the people. All I want to be is a potter. I want to live in my home and have no debt, no mortgage. I want to devote myself to pottery."

He wanted to spend his life creating pottery, yet he was in a sales position, selling computers over the telephone. Even so, he saw that he could be the best in sales, buy a house, and then pay off his mortgage in a fraction of the time his friends did, so he could live in that house mortgage free. He was sure his pottery sales would take care of his living expenses. So, while he wasn't able to integrate his passion at his job, he did see his job as a way to attain his goal of creating pottery, and that was a strong motivator.

By the way, Rob continued to be a top producer. Now, more than ten years later, he's paid the mortgage on his house and is creating pottery.

Liz Wants a Perennial Garden

Liz worked with Rob. A delightful young woman and a fantastic performer in sales, Liz also was a telephone sales representative by vocation and an artist by avocation. (In college, she had majored in music with a minor in art.)

One day we asked her, "If you had any amount of money that you needed, and if you had the time that you needed, what would you be doing?"

She replied, "I know exactly what I would do. I would plant the most beautiful perennial garden in Portsmouth, New Hampshire. I would have a perfect location, one of those hidden gardens downtown, and I would design and grow the most beautiful garden."

Liz expressed clearly what motivated her. After some creative thinking, we came up with the idea to decorate her workspace with the drawings she made of her future perennial garden. That way, whenever she became a little discouraged or lost a sale, she could look at her drawings and remember why she was a computer salesperson.

Another year of Liz's solid sales performance went by, and then one day she said, "The one thing that's missing in my life is time. I'm doing well, I can afford my perennial garden, but I don't have the time to plant and care for it."

Because Liz was clear about what she wanted to achieve in life, we used her need to come up with a solution. We started talking with other staff members, who were thrilled, and learned that many of them felt the same way she did: "Now I have the money, but I don't have the time." The company's solution was to initiate a sabbatical program. After five years of producing for the company, an employee received a three-month paid sabbatical. Liz used her sabbatical to start her garden.

On the surface, Rob and Liz seemed like unlikely people to be successful in a sales realm, but they were among the six top-tier sales producers at the company. Their stories show what can happen when you know what is important in your life. If Rob and Liz hadn't been clear about what was important to them in their lives, and if they hadn't seen their jobs as paths for achieving what they wanted, we would have lost them as salespeople. Instead, they were among our best sales performers while successfully achieving their personal goals. By knowing what is important to each individual, a company can support a person's goals in the workplace.

MAKING A DIFFERENCE

Two dear college friends, a husband and wife whom I, Alesia, don't see that often, traveled across the country to visit me. They brought along their three daughters, ages nine, twelve, and thirteen. I looked forward to spending time with them and enjoying their company. I wanted them to have a wonderful memory of this trip. Unfortunately, I hadn't foreseen the logistics of having an additional five people in the house. I found myself running around to make sure they all had towels and sheets, food and snacks, and their favorite drinks and coffee.

When we would all sit down to enjoy a meal together, I found myself constantly bouncing up from the table to get something out of the oven, or the refrigerator, or to replace a napkin. My friends would plead, "All that can wait, just come, sit down and join us." But I couldn't sit still, because there was so much to do.

I could feel my anxiety building up as I tried to be present with them and at the same time be a good host. I wanted to make sure I had things for the children to do, that the house was always picked up, that meals were served hot, and that the kids had snacks ready when they needed them. In all of my frantic activity, I wasn't enjoying the visit.

So I stopped and asked myself, "What is important here?" That simple act of stopping allowed me to get in touch with why I was doing what I was doing and with what truly mattered to me. I ran around like a crazy lady because I wanted everyone to have a good time and to make sure that the young ones were entertained and cared for.

Yet what I was yearning for was to spend "quality" time *being* with my friends and their children so that we could reconnect. I wanted to have long, delicious conversations by the fireplace and play board games with the children; to take long, leisurely walks and play hide-and-seek with the kids.

I began to realize that my true intention was to create a glorious memory of the visit for my guests and me and to spend as much time with them as possible. That's the difference I wanted to make. All that running around I was doing wasn't making a difference in the quality of the visit. I began to chill out, relax, and savor my guests.

Here's another true story: I have a friend whose house was always immaculate. She had five kids and two dogs but you wouldn't know it. It didn't matter the day or the time, if you went to her house you would find everything in perfect order. One day, I went to visit and I was complimenting her on how dazzling the house was. She turned to me and said, "If I had to do it over again, I would not have spent so much of my time cleaning when the children were younger, because I realize now that it did not make a difference. What would have made a difference instead is if I had played more games with them or read more books with them or, better yet, listened to them more. That would have made a difference."

We all strive in some way to make a difference, and that drive is imprinted in us at an early age. Even two-year-olds want to contribute. They want to help. They want to be useful. They want to put the dish in the dishwasher. They want to put the sock in the drawer. They want to do something that has an impact. Since we are fundamentally wired to make a difference, we can use this propensity as a compass for how we conduct ourselves, how we create our lives, and how we engage in our daily interactions. How can you make a difference that makes a difference? What would make a difference, given what matters to *you* or what is important right now?

Now that you've looked at what you say is most important to you, let's take the next step and begin to create your life.

5

CREATING YOUR LIFE

The future is not some place we are going, but one we are creating. The paths are not to be found, but made. And the activity of making them changes both the maker and their destination.

—*JOHN SCHAAR*

Creating your life and taking your effectiveness to the next level is a lifelong pursuit. If it were only something to know or understand, then we would all be masters. However, much like other pursuits, such as golf, tennis, chess, or bridge, while knowing and learning are important, practice, practice, practice is the key.

One of the practices we advise, which has produced remarkable results for us, family members, friends, and clients, is to look out a year ahead and create your life as a series of accomplishments. First, choose the realms of your life that are important to you. Second, write what you want to accomplish in those realms. Last, picture what your life will be like a year from now, having accomplished what you set out to do, and write that down.

When we talk about accomplishments in this manner, we're not talking about the things that you have completed at the end of the day. We are looking at what you intend to accomplish in your life as a function of the things that you do every day. An example of an annual accomplishment is "I am fit, pleased with how I look, and enjoy exercising, eating healthy foods, and being in the best shape of my life." That's the overall accomplishment, but there are activities you need to do every day to fulfill that accomplishment.

RESOLUTION VS. ACCOMPLISHMENT

There is a difference between making a New Year's resolution and creating an accomplishment for the next year of your life. When people make resolutions, they usually look at themselves in the moment and try to find something they don't like, something they want to fix. They look at their careers, eating habits, lack of exercise, or smoking habit and think, "I'm going to fix it this time." They are forceful and resolute.

A resolution presupposes that you are broken in some way and need fixing or repairing; there would be no need for a resolution if you weren't broken. It presupposes that you have failed, because if you had fixed the problem before, you wouldn't need to bring out the big guns to fix it this time. A resolution is in some sense a last resort; if you don't make it happen this time, there is no hope left for you. Resolutions are loaded with negative connotations. They are ways of making yourself wrong about something you should have done. It is no wonder that we usually only keep them for three weeks. Resolutions set us up for failure. Four out of five people who make New Year's resolutions eventually break them, citing too much to do or lack of commitment as the primary reasons.[1]

When you create an accomplishment for the next year of your life, you look at an area, such as your career, and envision it a year from now. Begin by imagining that it is December 31st of next year. You are sitting across the table from a close friend, and you are toasting the New Year. You are saying, "Yes, it has been such a great year; here are all the wonderful things that happened to my career this year." You come at it from how it feels to have accomplished certain things over the year. The idea here is to write down what you accomplished and how you feel as a result of accomplishing it.

A resolution is concerned only with the outcome. The accomplishment contains the outcome, but is more interested in the process by which that outcome is achieved. When you create your life as a series of accomplishments, you consciously envision the most positive outcome of whatever endeavor you engage in. This is a creative act that requires intention and commitment.

There is no resoluteness with accomplishments created in this manner; there is only the feeling of success. You may write accomplishments such as, "I have been promoted to manager," "I have experienced international travel," and "I have been recognized for my work." Whatever your accomplishments may be, you enjoy the experience of having accomplished them. This creates forward momentum and choices for purposeful action.

CREATING YOUR LIFE ONE YEAR OUT

Musician Carlos Santana has said, "Most people live and die and they don't even know what their calling was. Maybe they didn't take the time to push the pause button. What happens when you find your calling—everything stops and you just see what you're supposed to do and why you're supposed to do it. When I heard the first guitar in Tijuana, it made me realize that I have possibilities and opportunities to discover and nothing was going to stop me."

The act of creating your life as you envision it one year from now is powerful because:

- You've incorporated what's most important to you.
- You've taken the long view, looking ahead to state what you will accomplish during that year.
- You've experienced today what it will be like when you have accomplished what you said you would one year from now.

Creating your accomplishments a year out is similar to the visualization techniques used in the sports world, especially by golf greats. The best players in the world get to know a golf course before they play it. They research it. They know every hole, the length of the hole, and the type of grass. They know the weather conditions for the day. They know which club is best for each circumstance. And yet, even though they know all that, when they stand at the tee before swinging their club, they stop. They will not tee off until they visualize the swing, the hit, and the full journey of the ball going where they want it to go. They visualize what it is going to be like when the ball lands precisely where they want it to, whether it's on the fairway, on the green, or into the hole.

FIVE STEPS TO CREATE YOUR ANNUAL ACCOMPLISHMENTS

When you create accomplishments a year out, you are tapping into the power of visualization and crafting your future life. Envisioning what has been accomplished and then creating the experience of what it is like being there is detailed in five steps:

1. Choose the important realms of your life.

2. List goals you want to achieve and outcomes you desire in each realm.

3. Create a summary accomplishment for each realm.

4. Share your accomplishments with others during the process, and use this as an opportunity to further refine your accomplishments.

5. Keep your accomplishments in the forefront.

STEP 1: EXAMINE THE IMPORTANT REALMS OF YOUR LIFE

In chapter 4, you did some exercises designed to support you in looking at what is most important to you. In this chapter, we ask you to list what is important to you in categories we call the realms of your life. Here are some realms you can use to jump-start this process:

- Family/Friends/Significant Other/Romance
- Health/Fitness
- Education/Personal Growth
- Finances/Wealth/Philanthropy
- Fun/Recreation/Sports
- Spirituality/Religion
- Business/Career
- The Arts/Music/Theater
- Community/Politics
- Home/Garden
- Professional Development

Look again at the list you made in chapter 4 and correlate what you say is important to you within these realms. You might find that you need to create your own realm if something that is important doesn't fit in the categories listed here.

To start, choose one of the realms and list what you want to accomplish by the end of the year. You might start by stating the specific goals you want to achieve by the end of the year, then visualizing what the results will look like or experiencing how you will feel when they are accomplished. There are several visualization and reflection techniques to help you create what your life will be like a year from now. Use the technique that works best for you.

Sample Chart of Accomplishments for Finances

In the example in table 5-1, the realm of importance is finances and we have listed five accomplishments.

Now, start your own list in a separate document. Fill in your list of accomplishments in one realm of importance. You can start with finance, as in the example, or you can start with any other realm you like. Create a list of accomplishments for each realm of your life.

Table 5-1. Chart of accomplishments for your realms of importance.

REALM OF IMPORTANCE: I ENJOY FINANCIAL SUCCESS	
Accomplishment 1	My student loans are paid off.
Accomplishment 2	I have added $1,500 to my IRA/401(k) account.
Accomplishment 3	My credit card debt is now 0.
Accomplishment 4	I have $500 in my home improvement fund.
Accomplishment 5	We have $1,000 in our vacation account.

STEP 2: ENHANCE THE ACCOMPLISHMENTS

Now, for each realm of your life, you should have a chart that lists your initial accomplishments. You might have six, ten, or twelve charts. In this step, you want to enhance your accomplishments. Review each realm of importance and start by answering a series of questions about each accomplishment you would like to achieve by the end of the year, to better understand what's in it for you and how you feel about it. The idea is to enrich the experience and add color to it. Use the following questions as a guide to assist in making your accomplishment more vibrant and real for you:

- How will you feel about yourself after completing this accomplishment?
- What strengths or resources will you need to call on to accomplish this achievement?
- What benefits will be made available to yourself and others by accomplishing it?
- What obstacles will you overcome to accomplish it?

A sample chart of accomplishments for finance, with enhancements added (in italics), is shown in table 5-2.

STEP 3: CREATE A SUMMARY ACCOMPLISHMENT

Now, write a paragraph-length summary of the accomplishments for each of your realms of importance. These summary paragraphs

Table 5-2. Realm of importance: finances.

REALM OF IMPORTANCE: I ENJOY FINANCIAL SUCCESS	
Accomplishment 1	**My student loans are paid off**—the day finally arrived and I did it! Now I get to keep more of my own money.
Accomplishment 2	**I have added $1,500 to my IRA/401(k) account** and I'm excited to be saving for my future again.
Accomplishment 3	I am relieved that **my credit card debt is now 0** and I am proud that we were able to stay focused over the year to make this happen.
Accomplishment 4	**I have $500 in my home improvement fund** and I am set up to succeed with my financial goals, because I have automated payments toward my account.
Accomplishment 5	**We have $1,000 in our vacation account.** A vacation to Ireland in 2012 is a reality.

are called your annual accomplishments, and they are what you are going to keep with you as your accomplishments for the year. So let's create a summary of your accomplishments for the realm of finances by writing a statement that expresses all aspects of the accomplishments. For example:

I enjoy financial success. My student loans are paid off, and I'm proud that I paid them off in a timely matter. I've added $1,500 to my IRA/401(k) account, and I'm excited to be saving for my future again. I'm relieved that my credit card debt is now zero, and proud that we were able to stay focused over the year to make this happen. I have $500 in my home improvement fund, and I'm set up to succeed with my financial goals because I've automated payments into my account. We have $1,000 in our vacation account, so a trip to Ireland is a reality in just two more years.

Now go through each of your realms and create a similar summary paragraph. When you finish, you will have a list of your yearly accomplishments. By repeating this process for the other realms of importance in your life, you create your summary chart of accomplishments, such as the one shown in table 5-3.

Table 5-3. Sample summary chart for finances.

REALM OF IMPORTANCE: I ENJOY FINANCIAL SUCCESS	
Accomplishment 1	My student loans are paid off—the day finally arrived and I did it! Now I get to keep more of my own money.
Accomplishment 2	I have added $1,500 to my IRA/401(k) account and I'm excited to be saving for my future again.
Accomplishment 3	I am relieved that my credit card debt is now 0 and I am proud that we were able to stay focused over the year to make this happen.
Accomplishment 4	I have $500 in my home improvement fund and I am set up to succeed with my financial goals, because I have automated payments toward my account.
Accomplishment 5	We have $1,000 in our vacation account. A vacation to Ireland in 2012 is a reality.
Summary Accomplishment	I enjoy financial success Now that my monthly bills are paid automatically, I can give my attention to creating new business rather than paying bills. By maxing out my IRA/401(k) contributions, I am ensuring funds will be available for our retirement. We are enjoying choosing and contributing to organizations and charities that support our stand for a just and sustainable world. And we're enjoying trips to parts of the world that were mere dreams before.

STEP 4: SHARE YOUR ACCOMPLISHMENTS

When sharing your accomplishments, we recommend you choose two or three people; for example, your spouse and one or two people with whom you work closely or have known for a long time. You are looking for people who know you well (at least in one realm of life) and who will freely comment on what you share with them. Speaking the accomplishments out loud is a powerful exercise because it makes them more real for you and facilitates feedback from people who are important to you. You might want to first rewrite your summary accomplishment several times until you are satisfied with it before reading your accomplishments aloud or sitting down and going through them with someone you trust.

Your list doesn't have to be complete or perfect. In fact, it may not be complete until you've shared it with several people. These accomplishments take on an additional richness when you edit and read them to someone else. Continue this process until you are satisfied with your accomplishments.

By creating your accomplishments, you are creating your intentions; you are creating your life in front of you. So, although we highly recommend that you share your accomplishments with selected others, we also recognize that these are *your* accomplishments and it is completely up to you if you want to make them known to other people.

STEP 5: KEEP YOUR ACCOMPLISHMENTS IN THE FOREFRONT

Now that you are clear about your accomplishments for the year, print them out and keep them in front of you. In chapter 8, we'll suggest ways to check in on your progress. For example, you can make an appointment with yourself each month to review and re-create your accomplishments. This simple action will keep the end-game in sight and also keep you open to resources and opportunities for fulfilling your accomplishments.

WALK YOUR TALK

The value of identifying what you want to accomplish in life is that it brings clarity and focus to what you choose to do or not do. Creating accomplishments for the next year of your life gives you the opportunity to fulfill what's most important. It allows your family, friends, and coworkers to partner with you in realizing these accomplishments. You've placed a marker for how your life will be in the future.

Now it's about designing your days to make this future happen. We've all heard the phrase "Walk your talk." That is the true test. You can say whatever you want to say in these exercises, but it's what you schedule in your calendar and what you do with your time that is the measure of living the satisfying and rewarding life you created.

EXAMPLES OF ACCOMPLISHMENTS

Health

- I am well nourished and fit. I feel good in my body. My movement is fluid and free, and I feel strong.
- I have reached the intermediate level in Pilates and jog three to four miles several times per week.
- My personal trainer and I meet routinely to discuss and modify my health and exercise plan.

Family and Friends

- My siblings and I worked together to assist our parents in moving to a retirement community in New England that's close to most of the family. We continue to realize what a gift it is for us to be with them.
- I thoroughly enjoy "Mondays with Sam." Being part of my grandson's life is such a privilege.

Community

- I became a committed recycler this year. This is my contribution to the planet. I have also educated myself to lead a greener life.
- I had a block party this summer. We closed down the street and had a great time. I am so happy to be connected to my neighbors.
- I have become a gardener this year. Trading seeds, plants, and growing advice with my family and neighbors has been an enriching experience. My garden produced enough over the summer that we

were able to can and freeze our favorites for ourselves as well as for holiday gifts.

Philanthropy

- I continued to support my friends and family in their charitable work as they did rides, runs, and other fund-raising activities.
- I have continued on as a board member of New Generation, a shelter for homeless pregnant women, making a difference in the lives of women and children at this most vulnerable time in their lives.

Fun

- I started getting books on CD from my local library. I order them online, pick them up, and have listened to many authors this year.
- As I continued to reach out to my community and friends, I entertained more this year by having a variety of folks to our home for fun, laughter, healthy food, and great conversations.

Business/Work Contribution

- I am energized by the work I do, and feel rewarded by it spiritually and financially.
- My organizational system works for me; things flow in and out effortlessly and I always have at my fingertips all the resources and information I need; my electronic devices support all my endeavors in a fun and creative way.
- I have established a strategic work plan for the year and reviewed it on a weekly basis, making changes as necessary on a quarterly basis.

Home

- My home is my sanctuary. I have renovated my office, kitchen, and both bathrooms.

Remember our motto: Create your life and design your days. Now that you have identified what is important and written out your annual accomplishments, you are ready to begin designing your days to live the life you create.

PART
THREE

THE MORE-TIME-FOR-YOU SYSTEM TO ORGANIZE YOUR WORK AND GET THINGS DONE

One can make a day of any size and regulate the rising and setting of his own sun and the brightness of its shining.
—JOHN MUIR

6

CAPTURING YOUR THOUGHTS

The shortest pencil is longer than the longest memory.
—*OLD PROVERB*

" A penny for your thoughts," a friend said the other day. Imagine if you were paid a penny for every thought you had in a day. That would add up to a handsome sum of money by the end of the year. Our thoughts are elusive. Their visits to our consciousness can be very brief. They come from out of nowhere and then retreat quickly. Most of our thoughts are fleeting and inconsequential, but some can have great consequence and are worth noting. The trick is to capture the thoughts that are noteworthy. This chapter introduces a practice that is central to your ability to have more time for you. It will allow you to "download" the thoughts that you want to remember and relieve you of having to expend energy trying to recall or locate where you've written something down. This practice brings a sense of well-being and peace of mind, allowing you to:

- Have a consistent place to keep track of what you need to do or want to do. No more hunting around your desk, office, car, or garage for reminders.

- See your calendar scheduled with tasks and activities that you want to do and that you say you will do.
- Have your arms around everything you say you will do—all of it. You'll experience the kind of peace of mind that comes from knowing you are not dropping the ball on anything, and from having control over everything that you say is important to you.
- Experience a newfound sense of freedom and powerfulness—the freedom that comes from you making the choices about what you do every day.
- Find ease in living the life that you want and experiencing the life of your dreams.

If you have ever taken on new daily practices, such as an exercise regimen or a diet program, you may remember that the first several days your old habits are screaming, "Go ahead and buy that bag of chips! Eat that cookie!" or "Stay in bed. You deserve the rest. You don't need to go to the gym today."

As with diet and exercise, after using the program for a week or so, you begin to feel the benefits. You become clearer about how much time you have to accomplish what you want. You begin to make choices based on what's most important to you as you see which habits and activities are displacing the time you need to do what is most important to you.

When we lead people through this process in a workshop or a coaching session, they share their experiences and discuss the process with others who are trying these new practices at the same time. You might find someone or a group that would like to undertake these new practices with you. Then you can share experiences among yourselves, discussing your difficulties as well as your successes.

CAPTURING EVERYTHING

Let's begin by getting a handle on everything in your life that takes time. Everything in your life includes all that you:

- Have on your mind
- Have to do
- Want to do
- Should be doing
- Don't want to do
- Forgot to do
- Want someone else to do
- Think would be a good idea to do
- Need to do
- Dream about doing
- Hate to do
- Love to do

You are working with new practices here that will allow you to include all of the things on your mind. While it may seem daunting, this crucial step brings a sense of control, peace of mind, and relief that you didn't think was possible. Don't fret; we'll take you through the process so that you can accomplish this task one step at a time.

One of the major impediments to our effectiveness and productivity is that our minds are too full of things that we know we should be doing or want to be doing, or things that we forgot to do. Dr. Edward Hallowell, MD, specializes in diagnosing and treating attention deficit disorder (ADD). In his book, *CrazyBusy,* he states:

Brain overload has reached the point where our entire society is suffering from culturally induced ADD. . . . Once applicable only to a relatively few, the symptoms of ADD now seem to describe just about everybody. People with untreated ADD rush around a lot, feel impatient wherever they are, love speed, get frustrated easily, lose focus in the middle of a task or a conversation because some other thought catches their attention, bubble with energy but struggle to pay attention to one issue for more than a few seconds, talk fast or feel at a loss for words, often forget where they're going or what they are going to get, have bright ideas but can't implement them, fail to complete what they're doing, have many projects going simultaneously but chronically postpone completing them . . . feel they could do a lot more if they could just get it together, get angry easily when interrupted, feel powerless over the piles of stuff that surround them, resolve each day to do better tomorrow, and in general feel busy beyond belief but not at all productive.[1]

Hallowell accurately describes the experience of life for many of us: "Your goal," he writes, "is to rein in your attention on what you want to accomplish and then identify the time to complete it."

Everyone suffers from undiagnosed, culturally induced ADD to one degree or another. There's more to it than just the psychology. So let's take a quick look at the *physiology* of what's happening in your brain, the one and only processor humans have, and look at the impact on you.

Let's begin with the right side of the brain. Its job is to intercept everything that's going on and absorb it like a sponge. The right side of the brain is in charge of incoming stimuli. It takes all this incoming data and sends it to the left side of the brain to sort and store for later retrieval so you can respond.

Social scientists have long assumed that it is impossible to process more than one string of information at a time. The brain just can't do it. And, much of the time, the left side of our brain cannot keep up with all the incoming information to respond fast enough. How many times have you suddenly remembered something that has nothing to do with what you're doing at the moment? We even have a phrase for it: "That came to me from out of the blue," or "out of nowhere." Well, it didn't. It came to you when your brain was finally able to catch up and produce a response.

There are limits to how much complexity humans can handle. At today's instantaneous pace, many of us have exceeded those moment-by-moment limits. Relief only comes by capturing everything on one list.

Culturally induced ADD causes fragmentation in our thinking, leaving us stressed or anxious as we go through our days. The easiest way to handle the distractions that cause anxiety is to start clearing your mind. The easiest way we've found to clear your mind is to empty it by *writing everything down* in one specific place that is always easily accessible and convenient to use.

Sales trainer Charlie Greer cites very interesting statistics produced by the National Science Foundation (NSF): "We think a thousand thoughts per hour. The average person thinks about 12,000 thoughts per day. A deeper thinker, according to this [NSF] report, puts forth 50,000 thoughts daily."[2] No matter how you look at it or count it, a great deal of thinking happens every day with many thoughts running across your mind. How do you keep up? How do you keep it all straight?

Well, rather than counting on your memory to store and retrieve items for you, we suggest you consistently capture as many of those thoughts and ideas as you can in one place. We looked at professionals and organizations in other fields—medicine, sports, education, and industry—that have developed best practices and adapted them into a model for our own effectiveness practices.

BEST PRACTICE: CAPTURE

Our first best practice comes from a well-known delivery service: FedEx. Packages from businesses and individuals from all over the country are dropped off or picked up by FedEx drivers, driven to the local airport, and flown that evening to one central location in Memphis, Tennessee. Within a matter of hours, all the packages are sorted and placed back on flights to their final destinations. When Fred Smith, the founder of Federal Express, developed this business model, people thought he was crazy. How could it be efficient to send packages from Boston destined for New York through Memphis, Tennessee?

We've seen the results. This approach revolutionized overnight delivery service and how packages are shipped daily. Today, most of the 3 million packages that FedEx delivers each day still go through Memphis.

We are going to use the FedEx model as an effectiveness practice for handling everything that comes at us each and every day.

Let's start by looking at how we keep track of all of our thoughts, ideas, and commitments right now. Use the checklist in table 6-1 to stimulate your thinking and list all the places you currently keep reminders of things to do. Write down every place and every technique, including the Post-it notes on your computer monitor, as well as the stacks of papers on your desk or the magazines piled in the corner.

Currently, you are probably not capturing all of your thoughts, and when you do, you most likely put them in any number of places. Sometimes you may put reminders in a couple of places at once so you can be sure you'll be able to locate them when you need them.

Table 6-1. Where do you keep everything now?

☑ Check off all the things you do to remind yourself of what you need to do:

- ☐ Post-it notes on my car windshield, refrigerator, computer monitor, or folders, etc.
- ☐ My to-do list(s) in a notebook, on a whiteboard, or on my computer, etc.
- ☐ Ask a friend, colleague, or coworker to remind me
- ☐ Notes on scraps of paper or business cards in the side pocket of my computer bag, briefcase, purse, or wallet
- ☐ Stacks of papers, envelopes, notebooks, folders, or newsletters on my desk
- ☐ Pop-up reminders on my home computer
- ☐ My "old" to-do list
- ☐ E-mails in my Inbox, Sent, or Draft folder
- ☐ Voice messages sent to myself
- ☐ Notes on folders, my hand, article margins, scraps of paper, backs of envelopes, backs of business cards, and napkins

- ☐ Appointment cards and business cards with notes on the back, on my desk, or in my purse/wallet
- ☐ Writing on my kitchen calendar
- ☐ My household projects list when I can find it
- ☐ Notices in my calendar for meetings long past
- ☐ My folder for bills to pay, thank-you notes to write, or expense statement to prepare, etc.
- ☐ Messages left on my cell phone voice mail, in my work and home voice mail
- ☐ E-mails to myself and e-mails that I think I'll get to someday
- ☐ The stack of magazines on the end of my desk
- ☐ Documents in my computer somewhere
- ☐ Other:

  _____

- ☐ Other:

  _____

Is this a system for success? Just think about the extra brain cycles it takes to remember where you put the thing you want to remember.

What if you could eliminate the need to have redundant systems to remember things? What if you could have one primary place to capture everything coming at you?

Rather than counting on your memory, you can use one of several different resources to capture your thoughts and ideas, including:

- Notebook (small, medium, or large) or steno pad or composition book
- Letter-size pad of lined paper (with or without clipboard)
- iPhone, BlackBerry, or other similar electronic device
- Digital voice recorder

We are going to use the term *capture tool* when referring to a notepad, tape recorder, a BlackBerry, and so on. It's not because we want to rename the thing you already know and use; it's because we want you to realize that this everyday item you may be carrying with you for many different reasons is now being used for a very specific purpose with a specific set of practices.

When things come to mind during the day that you may want to do later, write, type, or record them immediately. Write down thoughts, requests, ideas, errands, dreams, promises, goals, insights, gift ideas, and observations—anything that comes to mind.

Keep your capture tool with you all day. During the day, you may find that you get some of these items done. Great. In that case, cross them off or delete them. Our goal is to keep our mind working on what we say we want to accomplish. So every time something comes to you, write it down, even if you think you will get it done that day.

Using a capture tool is the first step in:

- Getting your arms around everything that there is for you to do and handle
- Eliminating that sneaking feeling that you forgot something important

- Reducing the stress that comes from hunting for that phone number at the last minute
- Having more personal and family time

We realize that we are asking you to put aside your thoughts about your current way of doing things and take on something new. We know how tough this can be, especially for people who already have a good system in place. This brings to mind a woman in one of our workshops who stood up with her large (9″ × 12″) Day-Timer Planner clutched to her chest, saying, "You can't take my Day-Timer away from me. *Everything* is in it. I wouldn't know what to do without it."

She's right. We weren't asking her to get rid of her Day-Timer or to stop carrying it around. What we were asking her to do was to choose and implement a separate capture tool for that week.

We're asking you to do the same thing: Use your capture tool to capture the ideas, thoughts, and requests that you need to remember as they come at you throughout the day.

The reason we strongly encourage you to keep a capture tool separate from your portable planning system is to give you a fighting chance to develop a habit of capturing and releasing each day. Our experience is that when a capture tool is embedded in a portable planning system, it's more difficult to take on these new practices. We understand it may be difficult for some people. Trust us on this one. It is best to use a small separate device to write down everything that comes to mind that you want to remember during the day.

Keeping Your Device Available

It is important that your chosen device becomes a constant companion. In the beginning, it can be a little difficult to remember to carry it with you all the time. But think of the things that you have become used to bringing with you always. For some of you, it may be your cell phone. Do you ever go anywhere without it? For others, it may be your keys or wallet. For others, it may be your purse, briefcase, or backpack.

Do not leave your home without your capture tool. Why? Because all day long you are thinking of things that you want to do, or need to do, or forgot to do. These thoughts keep coming, everywhere you go. What do you do with these thoughts now? If you are like most people, you barely notice them. And then, when a thought stirs you to action, you may react by:

- Saying to yourself, "Oh, I'll remember that later."
- Grabbing a handy scrap of paper and (if you have a pen or pencil) writing a note so you won't forget it.
- Asking someone who is with you to remind you.
- Writing it on your hand.
- Leaving yourself a message on your voice mail.
- Asking a friend to send you an e-mail to remind you.

If you don't write down your thoughts right away, you will tend to forget them. But if you do write them down, you have a better chance of retrieving them when you want, especially if you write them down in a reliable place where you know you can find the information, a place you've consciously chosen.

Now we all know this works because we already do it—for example, when there is something that we don't want to forget before we leave the house. How many of you place items in the car the night before, or next to the front door, or at the top of the stairs, so you'd have to trip over them before you forgot them? I, Rosemary, can remember the night before I was leaving on a two-week trip and needed to leave the house at 5:00 a.m. to catch an 8:00 a.m. flight. I was lining items at the top of the stairs that I didn't want to forget:

- A gift for the person I was staying with
- Workout instructions
- Bag of energy bars
- Vitamin container
- Bills to mail on my way out the door
- My itinerary
- Airline tickets

My husband stopped and asked me, "What is this cast of characters on the top of the stairs?" I looked at it all. I hadn't been aware of how much I relied on putting something where I could not miss it on the way out the door. But we do it, and it works. Why? Because we choose a reliable place to put everything. For the same reason, your new capture tool is also a reliable place to put things.

BEST PRACTICE: RELEASE

Throughout the day you've been capturing to-do items, ideas, things you promised to do for others, things other people promised to you, and so on.

As you look at your list at the end of the day, you'll see some of the items were already completed and you can cross them off. So far so good. Next, let's deal with all the unfinished business—the items that you were unable to complete during the day.

For this task we use the model of the hospital emergency room and its triage process. Triage was initiated in World War I, on the battlefields in France. Today, it's used in hospitals and trauma centers throughout the world to categorize or prioritize patients as:

- The deceased
- The injured who can be helped by *immediate* transportation
- The injured whose transport can be *delayed*
- Those with *minor* injuries who need help less urgently

After choosing how each patient is to be handled, doctors or nurses place them in holding areas or mark their ID bracelets with color-coded labels, indicating their triage categories.

We are going to use a similar approach as we take you through a step-by-step process that will leave you with an empty capture tool—one that is cleared of all items and ready to be used again tomorrow. At the end of the day, you have to review what you wrote down or recorded in your capture tool, and then identify the items that you were not able to complete during the day. You then open your calendar and schedule a time to do them.

You may notice some items you captured but didn't schedule.

These leftover items are the ones that you have not yet scheduled and not yet completed.

What are you going to do with this unfinished business? If you want to clear your mind and use it for something other than a memory pad, you are going to need to have a place for these items. The point of triage is to make quick but purposeful decisions. For the items in your capture tool, you must take one of three actions:

- Delete it.
- Do it.
- File it.

Before you can begin to triage, you need to set up a system that makes it quick and easy to do, one that gives you the assurance that you won't forget (or have to remember), so you can keep your thoughts on what you are doing rather than worrying about what you are forgetting to do.

CREATING TRIAGE FOLDERS

Using an e-mail and calendar system such as Microsoft Outlook is a convenient way to implement this triage system. First, create two new folders named:

- Waiting for Response
- Someday

If you've never created new folders, you can get help in Outlook or follow these instructions: In any view (such as Mail or Calendar), open the File List navigation pane on the left.

1. Highlight "Personal Folders."

2. In the Outlook toolbar, select "File."

3. Highlight "New."

4. Click on "Folder."

5. The Create Folder dialog box opens. Enter your new folder name, "Waiting for Response," and click OK.

Figure 6-1 shows a screenshot of this process. Repeat the same steps to create a folder for "Someday."

Figure 6-1. Setting up a "Waiting for Response" folder.

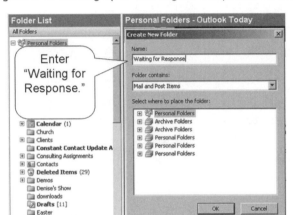

Triage Step 1: Delete It

This step actually has two parts:

• Cross off or delete any items you already completed.
• Cross off or delete those items you wrote down but that you are not committed to doing.

One of life's most satisfying acts can be taking out that list and crossing off the items that you completed during the day. It leaves you with at least a temporary sense of accomplishment. However, you also have to look at the items on your list and spot the ones that you will not even attempt to do—the ones that leave you wondering, "What was I even thinking when I wrote that down?" You cross them off your list, too.

Now let's deal with everything else on your list.

Triage Step 2: Do It

When you capture information you're not always thinking about why you are capturing it. Some of the things you write down will be notes and information you want to save. Some will be actions you can and want to take. For everything on your list that is an action item, there's a decision point. Here is an overview of the steps.

- Anything you can complete in less than two minutes: Do it now.
- If you are committed to doing it and it will take more than two minutes, pull out your calendar and schedule a time to do it.
- If you are committed to doing it, but can't schedule a time just yet because you need further information from someone before you can do it, post it to the Waiting for Response folder.

Doing It Now

If it will take less than two minutes to complete the item, just do it. Yes, right now. Get it off your list and off your mind. First, it's done, and second, you don't have to remember to do it, deal with it, or do it later. It's simply done.

Scheduling It Now

For every item on your list that is going to take more than two minutes to accomplish but that you are committed to completing, take out your calendar and schedule a time for it. Repeat this process until everything you are committed to doing is scheduled. By scheduling into your calendar everything you say you want to get done, you are automatically set up to remember to do it. Figure 6-2 is an example of placing some items from your capture tool into your calendar.

Waiting for Response

You are probably going to find that there are some items you want to do and are committed to do, but can't schedule yet because you

Figure 6-2. Scheduling items into your day and week.

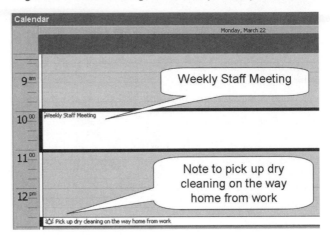

need some information from someone else before you can schedule it. Take each of these items and post a note in your Waiting for Response folder. Here is how to make the post:

1. Click on the Waiting for Response folder.

2. Go to "New."

3. Open the menu by clicking on the down arrow to the right of "New."

4. Choose "Post in This Folder."

5. Enter your note on the subject line and click "Post," which brings up a form.

6. Enter your subject, write your note, and click post.

Figure 6-3 shows where to find "Post in This Folder" in Microsoft Outlook. Clicking on "Post in This Folder" opens a new window (shown in Figure 6-4) where you can type in details about the item you are waiting for and from whom.

Think of this folder as a temporary holding folder. The only items that go in here are the ones you need or want to do but can't because you are waiting for someone else's input before you can

Figure 6-3. Posting a note in your Waiting for Response folder.

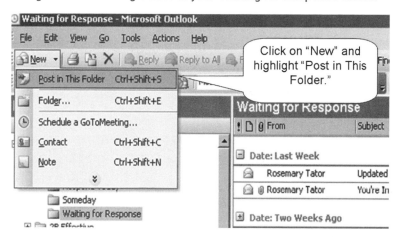

Figure 6-4. Post in this folder.

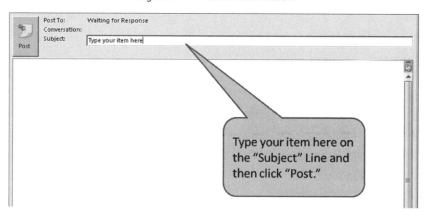

schedule. You want to view items in this folder at least once a day. Reviewing them at the end of the day allows you to:

1. Delete the items that have been handled during the day.

2. Choose to remind someone who hasn't responded with a call or message.

3. Let it wait another day.

Triage Step 3: File It

You need to find a place to put everything else that you haven't deleted or committed to do. If it is something you want to save, place it in an existing file or create one. If it's something you may want to save just because you never know if you'll need it, but you don't want to take the time to create a file for it, post a note in your "Someday" folder in Outlook.

During the day, some of the items you collect may be hardcopy items, such as brochures, programs, invitations, and so on, that you want to keep. File them. If you have an existing file folder that is appropriate, place them in there, or if you choose, use a new folder.

You may want to store some of the items in your capture tool in an electronic file format. If you have an existing folder, post a note to that folder, or if you choose, create a new electronic folder and post to that one.

Your Someday Folder

As you continue to triage items from your capture tool, you may find there are some items left over. These are items that you have chosen not to do anything about now and for which you don't find it worthwhile to create a separate file folder. However, you aren't ready to let them go, either. Place them into your hardcopy or electronic Someday folder.

Your Someday folder is a place to store all of the thoughts and tasks that you want to keep on your radar but aren't ready to schedule in your calendar. The purpose of the Someday folder is to free your mind from being worried that you will forget something or that it will fall through the cracks. By capturing these items and putting them in this one folder, you know right away where to find them. No more rummaging through multiple folders or searching through files. Anything you want to do, need to do, would like to do, and so forth, is either scheduled in your calendar or filed in your Someday folder. Anytime you want to resurrect an item or look at it, you can. The key is to continually empty your mind. Keep it clutter free by recording the things that come to mind. Then choose what you will do by scheduling in your calendar the items that you say are most important and putting the others in your Someday file.

We want you to place items in this folder, knowing that they are easy to find, review, and retrieve. We don't want this list to become your taskmaster—something that presses on you, urges you to do more, or makes you feel overwhelmed.

As with your Waiting for Response electronic folder, you may find that it is useful to color-code and categorize items in your Someday folder. The difference is that you don't need to review your Someday folder every day. This is a folder you may choose never to review again. Items in this folder are ones you have chosen not to do anything about, except keep them around for a while.

That's it. You have now learned how to handle every item that you captured today. Is every item crossed off? If yes, tear it out and throw the list away. Why not? You really are done with it. You should look forward to throwing the list away each day. Of course, some people cross everything off but still want to keep the list around "just in case." Instead of turning over another page and keeping the list in your capture tool, we recommend you still tear it out, but instead of throwing it away, place it in a hardcopy "monthly capture" file folder if it's too difficult for you to throw it out. There is nothing remaining in your capture tool. It's empty and ready for tomorrow.

GETTING STARTED

In this chapter you learned the value of freeing your mind to think about more important matters than remembering to drop off the dry cleaning. You learned to record everything on your mind in one easily accessible and convenient-to-use capture tool, rather than using multiple reminders in multiple places to try to remember something. By keeping your capture tool with you throughout the day, you can continually write down and add all thoughts and ideas as they come to mind. Then, before the end of the day, empty your capture tool using the triage method.

The capture and release practices are the heart of our system to organize your work and get things done. These practices allow you to download what's on your mind and keep track of everything important that you need to do or want to do. To begin your practice of capture and release, select a capture tool that is convenient for you. The most popular ones we see in use are notebooks (small, medium, or large), steno pads, or composition books; letter-size pads of lined paper (with or without clipboard); iPhone, BlackBerry, or similar electronic devices; or digital voice recorders. We recommend using your smartphone as your capture tool only when you can enter information into them very quickly. That way your fingers can keep up with your thoughts.

Next, keep your capture tool handy so that you can write down or record thoughts that you want to remember as they come up throughout the day. No more writing on the back of napkins, Post-it notes, or random slips of paper. Everything is collected in your capture tool. If you forget your capture tool, go back and get it. It is essential to discipline yourself to capture in one place the thoughts that come to mind. At the end of the day, release what you've collected by using the triage system. Either:

• Do it.
• Delete it.
• File it.

Have fun with this new practice and experience the peace of mind that comes from knowing that nothing is falling through the cracks.

7

DESIGNING YOUR DAYS

How we spend our days is of course how we spend our lives.
—ANNIE DILLARD

In the television series *Dirty Sexy Money*, actor Donald Sutherland plays a multibillionaire named Tripp. One of the episodes showed a morning in his life. The scene opened with someone pulling back the curtains with great gusto, welcoming in the daylight. Then the camera panned to Tripp lying in his bed (it was the butler who had opened the curtains). In the next scene, the butler gave Tripp a shave, handed him a tie, and then handed him the newspaper as he walked out the door. Wouldn't it be great if we all had a butler?

USING YOUR CALENDAR TO ASSIST YOU

Your calendar can be your butler, or if you prefer, your office assistant. Of course, your calendar can't open the curtains for you or hand you the newspaper, but it can remind you of an appointment.

Similar to what a butler may do, many calendar applications have a reminder function that serves as an alarm to inform you of what's next on your schedule or approaching soon. Until you have the services of an actual butler, your alarm can serve as your virtual butler. Here are a few examples of what using the reminder feature on the calendar can do for you.

When you write a description of what you want to accomplish during a period of time in your calendar, you can set an alarm to go off before the event to remind you that it's coming up. It's like having your butler announcing that your next appointment is due to begin in fifteen minutes. This gives you time to wrap up what you're doing and prepare for your next appointment

When you write the description of your appointment in a way that includes why it is important to you (perhaps relating it back to your annual accomplishments), you can create a sense of interest and perhaps even excitement for what you are about to do.

The reminder, when announced, tunes you into how this is yet one more event in your life that allows you to fulfill something that you say is important to you, and in ways that are consistent with the design of your life.

So the reminder and how you write it can be like a butler's service. Taking it further, imagine the butler announcing, "Madam, in fifteen minutes, your staff meeting is about to begin in room 205." So madam says, "Thank you, James. I can see it's time to finish wrapping up my interview with the possible new employee. I'll be there." Now picture James holding out a briefcase that has all the papers that madam needs to take to the meeting with her. "Thank you, James."

While there are many different software programs that provide calendars with an alarm function, figure 7-1 uses Microsoft Outlook, which is one of the most prevalent programs, to demonstrate how to use the reminder feature.

Open your calendar and double click on the date and time you would like your appointment to start. In the "Subject" line, name your appointment. Set the appointment end time and then check the box next to "Reminder." Use the pull-down menu to choose how

Figure 7-1. Setting a reminder alarm in your calendar.

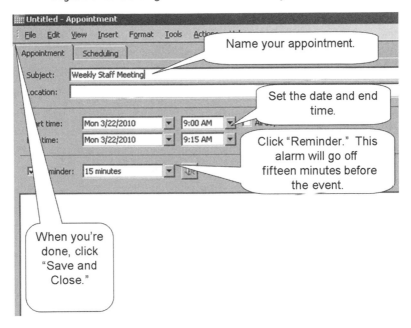

many minutes before your appointment you would like the alarm to go off, then click "Save and Close."

You can choose when you want to be reminded (such as in five minutes, eighteen hours, or two weeks before). For example, try using this feature to remind yourself about family birthdays two weeks before their date. Leave the birthday entry on the actual date, but set the alarm to be reminded in time to buy the card and gift and mail them.

It's nice to relate to your calendar as though it were your very own "James." You can set up your calendar so that it anticipates what's next for you, just like a butler would, and what you want to accomplish.

"Madam, here is your reminder. Your meeting is approaching."
"Oh, yes, thank you, James. I am off to my meeting now."
"Sir, your anniversary is approaching."
"Yes, thank you. I'll order roses so they are ready for me to pick up on my way home."

Everything that you need to know about the occasion (date, time, location, directions, who's attending) or need to have (report, notes, spreadsheet) for the meeting is already embedded in your calendar.

Figure 7-2 is an example of an appointment for a staff meeting. Notice the icons in the white area for notes. These are documents that are needed for this meeting—a Word document, an Excel spreadsheet, and a PowerPoint presentation. If you need hard copies of these documents to distribute during the meeting, you would schedule the time to make the copies beforehand.

To insert a file into your appointment (see figure 7-3) click on "Insert," then "File." You can then browse through your document folders to select the file you want to include. When you click on "File," the "Insert File" dialog box opens, bringing you to "My Documents" (see figure 7-4). Click on the folder you need to access the document you want.

You have choices about how you want the inserted file to appear as well (see figure 7-5). After you highlight your document, click on the Insert drop-down menu and choose text, attachment, or hyperlink.

You can also insert e-mail messages. They are referred to as

Figure 7-2. Inserting essentials into your calendar.

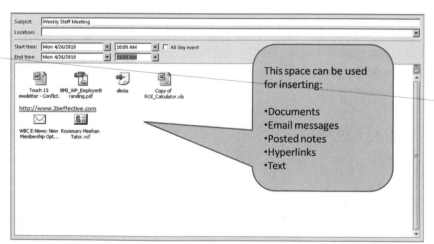

Figure 7-3. Inserting a file into your appointment.

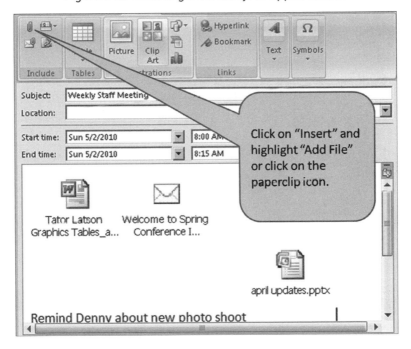

"items." Return to the Insert menu (figure 7-3) and choose "Item" this time, rather than "File." This action brings you to your inbox, where you choose the message you want to insert. You have the same choices available as to how you would like to insert (text, attachment, or hyperlink).

YOUR CALENDAR—A VIEW INTO YOUR LIFE

We each have twenty-four hours a day—168 hours a week—no more, no less. To be most effective with those hours, we need to know how we are actually spending our time, as opposed to how we think, hope, or want to spend our time. This is why we say that the first step in using your time most effectively is living out of your calendar and having it reflect your actual day.

Figure 7-4. Browsing your document folders to select a file.

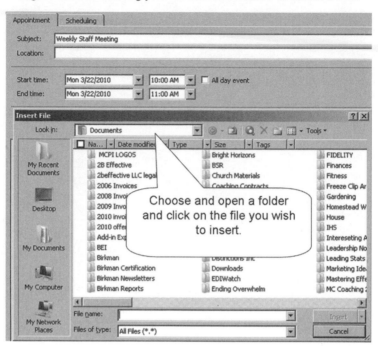

Here is another way to look at it. What if you are at the furniture store and you see this great hutch for $500. You want it, so you take out your checkbook (which hasn't been balanced) and say to yourself, "I think I have about $500 in there." You write the check for $500, only to find out the next day when you checked your balance there was only $300 in your account. Now you are overdrawn and living with the penalties and consequences. This analogy holds for how we manage our time. We often overdraw our "time account" by thinking we have more time than we do. Is it any wonder we run out of time to get things done? Or that we can't find the time to do what we really want?

Trying to chart your course without a map, without radar, and without weather reports leaves you in a state of urgency and emergency, with too much to do and not enough time to do it.

The more you are aware of what you do in a day, the more realistic you can be about what you want to accomplish. And the

Figure 7-5. Choosing a file format to insert into your appointment.

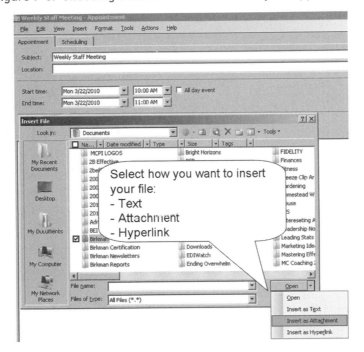

more you are aware of what you want to accomplish with the time you have, the more effective you will be with your time. We've found that planning for every hour in your day, even if the plan is to sit and do nothing, makes you more accountable for where the day went.

We are now going to include time on your calendar for the routines of your life—from the mundane to the inspiring. These are all the things you do each week. They are the patterns that take up a good part of your day. They are things you probably never schedule. Why? Because you don't need to be reminded to do them, and you've been treating your calendar as a reminder machine. We're now asking you to use your calendar for a whole lot more. We are asking you to live your life out of your calendar, so you'll be set up to do what you say is most important.

Some activities are so automatic that we discount their importance and tend to discount the fact that they take time. This is part of the mischief we create for ourselves when managing our time. We spend a considerable amount of time doing routine tasks that we never account for and then we wonder, "Where did the day go?"

Blocking Your Time

Start by blocking your time for the routines and rituals you do daily and weekly. Let's take a look at one part of your day, your weekday morning routines, so you can see what we mean. What are your patterns around morning routines? They might be shower and dress, exercise, meditate or pray, eat breakfast, wake up children and help them get ready for school, walk the dog, feed the cat, check e-mail, and so on. Of course some days may be different. Perhaps you exercise three mornings a week, not five; or perhaps you bring your children to school or daycare only on specific days. Even so, you choose how long the morning routines take, then block that time in your calendar.

Next, what are your patterns for when you first get to work? For example: Boot up your computer, get coffee, meet with cowork-ers, and handle your e-mail and voice mail.

What are your patterns during the day at work? You likely do such things as check your e-mail and voice mail at several different times, attend routine meetings, write routine reports, set aside time for phone calls, respond to customers, and then there's lunch.

What are your patterns when you leave work and head home? By this we mean activities such as commuting, grocery shopping, preparing meals, picking up the kids, eating, spending time with the children and your significant other, or tending to your hobbies, making phone calls, reading, watching television, and the like.

No one seems to have enough time. Yet everyone has 168 hours each week—all the time there is. Let's identify what you do with your 168 hours. Use tables 7-1 and 7-2 to assist you in identifying how much time you spend on certain activities and routines in your personal and work life.

To complete the charts, look at each activity and estimate how much time you spend each day and how many days you spend each

Table 7-1. Estimating your personal time.

PERSONAL TIME THINGS TO DO	HOURS PER DAY	DAYS PER WEEK	TOTAL HOURS WEEK
Sleeping			
Eating—preparing meals, cleaning up			
Shopping—food, clothes, etc.			
Children—reading, playtime, homework			
Spouse or Partner—time alone or dating			
Family and Friends—visits, outings, phone calls			
Play, Fun, Entertainment—movies, sports, theater			
Play, Fun, Entertainment—TV, games, hobbies			
Education and Personal Growth—classes, webinars			
Financial—paying bills, budgeting, investing			
Maintenance—houseclean, lawn work, laundry			
Maintenance—car, computer, other devices			
Health and Fitness—exercise, biking, etc.			
Personal Care—showering, dressing, etc.			
Reading and Writing—magazines, newspapers			
Spiritual—prayer, meditation, attending services			
Travel Personal—errands, family events			
Other			
Other			
Other			
Other			
Grand Total			

week engaged in that activity. Starting with personal activities, you will find that you do some activities each day of the week. For instance, you may sleep eight hours a day, seven days a week, for a total of fifty-six hours. Other activities might not happen on a daily basis, but a few times a week. For instance, your exercise routine could be one hour a day, three days a week, for a total of three hours a week.

When you have completed entering your time estimates, multiply the hours per day by the days per week and enter your total hours for that activity each week. Then tally your "total hours per week" column. The total represents the estimated amount of time you spend on personal activities each week.

Using the same process as above, complete the chart in table 7-2 to calculate the amount of time you estimate you spend on work activities.

Now add your total personal hours and your total work hours. Are they greater than or less than 168 hours?

Table 7-2. Estimating work time.

WORK TIME THINGS TO DO	HOURS PER DAY	DAYS PER WEEK	TOTAL HOURS WEEK
Meetings			
Conference Calls			
Phone Calls			
E-mail			
Reports			
Administration			
Travel			
Project Work			
Social			
Other			
Other			
Other			
Other			
Grand Total			

TRACKING HOW LONG ACTIVITIES TAKE

Now that you've calculated how long you *think* these activities take, it's time to match the plan to the actual time spent. Create a time log similar to the one shown in table 7-3. For the next three days, track how you actually spend your time. Try to be as specific as you can without being handcuffed to your time log. Notice and record the following information:

- How many activities in your week took more than the amount of time you estimated in the personal time and work time charts?
- How many activities took less time than you estimated?
- How many activities did you engage in that you didn't account for in your time log?

We predict that looking at the reality of how you actually spend your time will be sobering. But what does all this time estimating and logging have to do with your year and the life that you created to be one of accomplishment and fulfillment? Well, once you become clearer about how much time you have left in your life (after your routines), you will find it easier to make the choices that are aligned with what you want to accomplish. You will naturally become more discriminating about how you spend your time. You will find yourself choosing to do what matters the most.

By now you are beginning to account for how your day really proceeds, hour by hour. Next, let's look at scheduling practices that optimize your available time.

EFFECTIVE SCHEDULING TECHNIQUES AND PRACTICES

We've chosen a few scheduling techniques to assist you in designing your days with intention and purpose. These practices further support you in treating your calendar as your virtual butler, serving up the activities and appointments of your day. Using your calendar to

Table 7-3. Sample log for tracking your time

TIME	DESCRIPTION OF ACTIVITIES
6:00 AM	
6:30 AM	
7:00 AM	
7:30 AM	
8:00 AM	
8:30 AM	
9:00 AM	
9:15 AM	
9:30 AM	
9:45 AM	
10:00 AM	
10:15 AM	
10:30 AM	
10:45 AM	
11:00 AM	
11:15 AM	
11:30 AM	
11:45 AM	
12:00 PM	
12:15 PM	
12:30 PM	
12:45 PM	
1:00 PM	
1:15 PM	
1:30 PM	
1:45 PM	
2:00 PM	
2:15 PM	
2:30 PM	
2:45 PM	
3:00 PM	
3:15 PM	
3:30 PM	
3:45 PM	
4:00 PM	
4:15 PM	
4:30 PM	
4:45 PM	
5:00 PM	
5:30 PM	
6:00 PM	
6:30 PM	
7:00 PM	

guide you through the demands of your life is one of the keys to getting more time for you.

Creating Fifteen-Minute Segments

As you begin entering what you will do in your day in your calendar, you may find it useful to have fifteen-minute segments in your calendar, rather than the default thirty. With more segments in your calendar, you can enter more information about what you are doing. You can set up these segments by right-clicking anywhere on your calendar day and, under "Other Settings," choosing fifteen minutes from the "time scale" menu.

Using Color Labels

Color-coding is a useful way to get a quick view of daily, weekly, or monthly activities of a specific type or realm. Some of the ways we have found people differentiate the color by are:

- Accomplishments—one color for each realm
- Travel (to and from work or between appointments)
- Meetings
- Phone calls
- Family time

If you want to create your own labels rather than use the preset labels provided in Microsoft Outlook for the color-coding, click on the "Calendar Coloring" icon at the top left of your screen (next to the delete icon) and follow the directions for editing.

Handling Interruptions, Distractions, or Emergencies

Interruptions, distractions, and emergencies are part of our life and day, and we need to allocate time for them. One strategy to reduce the impact that interruptions and emergencies have on our schedule is to do a preemptive strike and schedule time for them in advance.

For example, if you have set aside 9:30 a.m. to 10:00 a.m. each morning for "interruptions and distractions," chances are you probably won't be interrupted the entire time. You may not be interrupted at that time at all. However, you probably can count on a half hour of interruptions, distractions, or emergencies before noon. What you've done by allocating this time is to keep yourself on schedule. After all, airlines "pad" the actual amount of travel time a flight takes in order to increase the chance that they will arrive on time; likewise, you can increase your chances of staying on schedule when you account for the inevitable interruptions, distractions, or emergencies that happen in your life each day.

When we don't account for this time, we:

- Miss deadlines
- Work longer to meet deadlines
- Feel overwhelmed by how much there is to do in so little time
- Aren't satisfied with what we produced or accomplished each day
- Become frustrated and upset with the interruptions

Each of these conditions only adds to our stress. So, at some basic level, it is better if you start telling yourself the truth about what's actually going on in your life. Many of us are overly optimistic about what we can actually accomplish in any given day. Help yourself and include at least two appointments during the day for interruptions and distractions. What's the worst thing that could happen? You're not interrupted that much? Well, great, then you have some "free" time. What could be better?

Figure 7-6 depicts a way to set an appointment for interruptions. When you enter a description on the subject line, have fun and be creative. For example:

Interruptions and emergencies are happening. No stress here. I've made room for them in my life.

Select "Tentative" for "Show time as." That way, if you are on a common file server, others will see that your time isn't actually booked, it's just tentative, possibly making you available for a group meeting.

Do not set a reminder for this appointment either. There's no

Figure 7-6. Handling interruptions and emergencies.

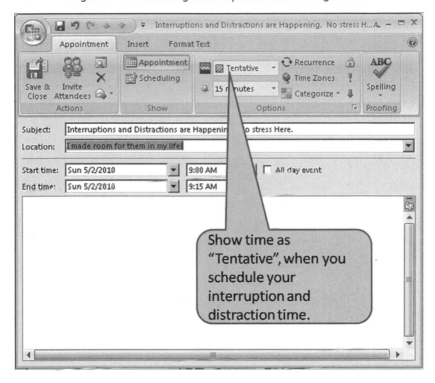

need to remind yourself to be interrupted, and you won't need to dismiss the reminder when it goes off.

Scheduling Transition Time

With our busy lives we often stop to do shopping and make pick-ups and drop-offs between work and home. This routine should be reflected in your calendar at the time you need to be doing it. Since you'll be in the car or on public transportation and not at your computer when you need to do these tasks, we suggest you make an appointment for the transition time and write all the stops you need to make and items you need to buy or drop off in the body of the appointment. In the subject line of the appointment, include a reminder to print out the details and take them with you. If your smartphone syncs with your calendar, you're all set.

Scheduling from the Outcome Backward

Another best practice we encourage you to incorporate that we find works well for projects and meetings comes from the sports world. Some of the best athletes in the world use this approach—great golfers in particular. Besides practicing, practicing, and practicing, studying the course, and analyzing his own swing, a great golfer like Phil Mickelson envisions how that ball will land in the hole. He thinks about the distance, the wind, the weather, and a myriad of other things. He envisions the ball moving from the tee into the hole. Then, and only then, does he address the ball and swing.

This practice works wonderfully for reaching our intended outcomes for projects and meetings. Visualizing what success looks like, and being clear about what the desired outcomes are, informs our actions. The perspective allows us to consider each action that needs to occur for us to reach the desired result. To illustrate, think of a project that you are about to begin or a meeting that you need to plan. Use the following questions to guide your planning.

- What is the outcome you intend to produce?
- What does it look like when it's complete?
- If it's a project, what's in it for you and for others?
- What needs to be done for your intended outcome to occur?

Looking at the answers to the above questions, what items do you need to schedule in your calendar? Now, schedule them in your calendar.

EFFECTIVE SCHEDULING INCLUDES YOUR FAMILY AS WELL

Many parents of school-age children are concerned about how to keep track of their children's schedules. Rather than keeping assorted notes or trying to keep track of your children's various activities and events in your head, use your calendar. Of course, you'll need a method for recording the children's appointments without interfering with or obscuring the view of other work or personal appointments you've already scheduled. This technique also works for coordinating schedules with a spouse or appointments when caring for aging parents.

Using the "All Day Event" Feature

One method that works well is to use the "all day event" feature. Begin by right-clicking anywhere on your calendar to open an appointment form. If you want to be reminded that April is at soccer practice between 3:00 p.m. and 4:30 p.m., and that the school bus brings her to practice, and that your neighbor, Ann, brings her home to her house, where your spouse picks April up at 5:30 p.m., type in a reminder such as the one shown in figure 7-7.

If you have several children with different schedules, you may want to choose a different color for each one. Figure 7-8 shows how the appointment looks on your calendar, with the note about April within your view all day, but without obscuring the rest of your schedule. If you have several children with various schedules, you can see how much stress and concern this can save. It's a lot quicker and easier to look at the top of your calendar when you get a call from your spouse asking, "What time did you want me to pick April up—or was it Tammy?"

There are a few more items to take care of to make sure April is set:

Figure 7-7. Tracking your children's schedules.

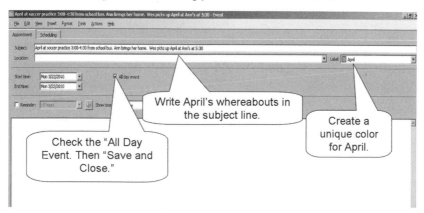

Figure 7-8. Using the "all day event" feature for your children's schedules.

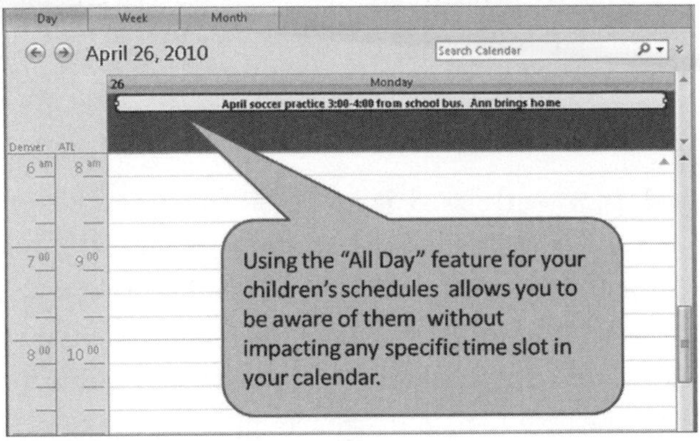

1. Make arrangements for Ann to take April home until your husband, Wes, arrives at 5:30 p.m.

2. Make arrangements for Wes to pick April up at Ann's at 5:30.

3. Remind April to bring her soccer gear to school in the morning.

You want to be able to take care of any outstanding items at the same time you are noting April's schedule. You want to think through all that needs to happen and account for it so that the details of April's afternoon are not weighing on your mind.

Items 1 and 2 on your list can be handled as e-mail, text messages, voice mail messages, or whatever method you find most effective. The key is to send that message or make that call at the same time you enter April's schedule. Then it's off your mind.

Item 3 is something for you to do or make sure is handled. Here are a couple ways to handle this task:

- Make it part of the morning checklist for your children.
- Set a reminder on your calendar next to your morning routines.

Figure 7-9 is an example of a morning checklist inserted into a calendar.

If you choose to embed a checklist in your morning routines, we suggest you set the appointment to recur after you insert the

Figure 7-9. Adding a morning checklist to your children's schedules.

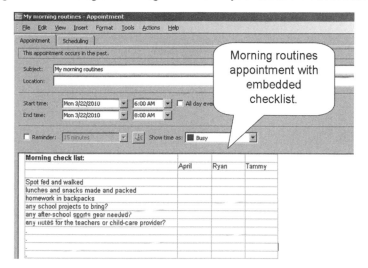

checklist, so it will carry through to every appointment. The point of the checklist is to get things off your mind and into a reliable system. Not only does it keep you from forgetting something or someone important, it frees you up to be more present in the moment with your children and family.

Communicating with Your Family Electronically

Although at first this practice might sound too businesslike, we have found that using the meeting request feature of Microsoft Outlook works very well when spouses or significant others use a computer or sync their phones or smartphones with their computer.

When you get an invitation or think of something you may want to do as a couple, instead of sending an e-mail message, send a meeting request with the date and time and with all the pertinent information in the body of the message to your spouse or partner. Put any notes about why you think it's a good idea in the body of the message. This way you are making it easy for them to look at the proposal and respond to the request. Your partner can even suggest something else for that time or another time for that event.

If you have teenage children, it is extremely useful to set a reminder to text them about specific appointments, such as:

- Dentist visits
- Taking out the trash and other chores
- Picking up their sister from Girl Scouts

One of my clients sets a reminder in her Outlook calendar for her child's 4:30 p.m. dentist appoint so she can text at 2:30 p.m., when the teenager is getting out of school and needs to see it.

SCHEDULING SUMMARY

When you are scheduling for effectiveness you are using your calendar to design the days of your life. This practice makes it possible to accomplish other results as well:

- Your schedule is now based on your "really available" time, rather than hoped-for time.
- You are able to account for the time you spend on the routines of your life.
- You have chosen what is most important for you to accomplish and scheduled enough time for you to complete those objectives.
- You have looked at your project or whatever you are out to accomplish from the outcome backward, being clear about what your end goal is even before you begin.
- You can be accountable to yourself and others for your promises and deliverables.

COACHING TIPS

To be successful at implementing these new scheduling practices: Pace yourself. Do not try to take on everything at once.

Keep in mind the old adage, "Inch by inch is a cinch." Commit to taking on one or two of the scheduling techniques. As you practice, you will develop new habits that will allow you to design your days so that you have more time for you.

The next chapter covers designing our weeks to ensure that we are considering our annual accomplishments, learning what worked and what didn't work in the previous week, and planning the week ahead.

8

DREAMS COME TRUE WHEN YOU PLAN

Go confidently in the direction of your dreams. Live the life you have imagined.

—HENRY DAVID THOREAU

No one can live your life but you. No one can create your life but you. In today's hyper-busy world, we often get so caught up in just catching up that we fail to take the time to live our lives.

In chapters 4 and 5, you took the time to reflect on what's most important in your life, and you used those findings to write out annual accomplishments to fulfill your dreams and goals—to, in effect, create your life a year in advance. In this chapter you'll learn a process to keep these dreams and goals alive for you each and every week.

LIVING INTO YOUR CREATED LIFE

Review and creation is a practice that you need to do each week. Schedule this weekly session with yourself for thirty to forty-five minutes. Choosing a time to review and plan is the critical practice for steering the ship of your life. Find a time when you are less likely to be interrupted. Many people have found that sometime over the weekend works best—Sunday evenings, for example, or some other quiet time. Guard and cherish this time.

The first step in your weekly review is an exercise designed to clear your mind, leaving you free to create next week and the rest of your life. To start, take out your capture tool (e.g., notepad, composition book, tape recorder, BlackBerry, etc.) and set a timer for ten minutes. Then write down or record anything that is top of mind for you. If you find yourself stuck after a few minutes, don't stop. Think about the different aspects of your life, such as work, home, family, or clubs, and your obligations or desires associated with each. For example, "I need to prepare the outline for the report that is due in two weeks," or perhaps, "I have to schedule an appointment with my dental hygienist." Something will come to mind; you can count on it. When you feel you have written down everything and completely cleared your mind, then refer to the questions in table 8-1 and either 1) write answers to each of the questions on a separate sheet of paper, or 2) write down or record anything that comes to mind as you mentally respond to these questions. The purpose of answering these questions is to provide you with an opportunity to track your progress and tune and correct.

We suggest you place these questions, and any others you find useful, in the body of your weekly review appointment in your calendar before you set the recurring appointment. This way these questions will always be where you need them, when you need them.

The weekly review is a time when you can catch up with yourself. It is when you catch those things that weren't completed at the end of the day, not because you didn't schedule time to do them, but perhaps because you didn't allow enough time for interruptions and emergencies, or you didn't schedule enough time to handle your e-mail and voice mail, or you didn't allocate enough time to handle a certain project. As we like to say, "Life happens."

It's also the time to see how your week correlated with your

Table 8-1. Weekly review questions.

1	**What did I accomplish?** How long did tasks take compared to the time you allocated for them? Do you want to "adjust" any time allocations you set for the coming week?
2	**What didn't you accomplish that you intended to? And why?** Where are those items now? In your calendar or "Someday" folder, or some other place? Have you scheduled them in your calendar for next week or month? Have you moved them to your Someday folder? Have you deleted them altogether? Make peace with all that you didn't do (time is still on your side). Pat yourself on the back for all that you did accomplish. You rock!
3	**What did you accomplish toward your newly created life?** Pull out your annual accomplishments and take a look. Which realms did you work on? Which ones weren't touched?
4	**Plan next week. Open your calendar and look at your week.** Are you still committed to doing what you previously scheduled? Do you need more or less time to complete any of the items in your calendar? Make the adjustment. Take out your preferred capture device (e.g., notepad, tape recorder, smartphone) and triage your scheduled tasks.

annual accomplishments. Which realms did you work on fulfilling and which were untouched?

For example, as you look through your realms, you may notice that last week you spent no time with family or friends. You pull out your calendar intent to rectify this oversight, look at the coming week, and see it's packed. Since you are committed to live the life you created, how are you going to include family and friends this week? Take the time now to see what tasks or appointments you can move on your calendar. Perhaps you can take advantage of being in one location where there is family close by or where you can meet with friends. Can you invite a family member or a friend to join you at an event that you are already scheduled to go to? If not this week, how about next?

For those of you who use Microsoft Outlook for your calendar, one way to easily see how much time you are spending living into your created life is to color-code your time. Select one color for each of your realms. Then, when you schedule the time to do something in that realm, it's easy to see. For example, if you want to track how much time you are spending on an area of accomplishment, look for the red, the yellow, or the green blocks of color-coded tasks or events.

Take a final critical look at your coming week. If you are seeing a week that's already full, look again; is there anything that you can move, delete, or delegate to someone else?

Choosing how your life proceeds is truly up to you. This can sound trite in today's cynical world, but consider that once you know what you want, you will be taking one step at a time to accomplish it. For example:

- How much money I have in the future is based on how much money I am saving today. (Do you have time in your calendar to manage your savings and investments?)
- How fat or thin I will be tomorrow depends on what I eat and how much (or how little) I exercise today. (How much exercise time do you have in your calendar?)

The first thing many diet plans recommend is tracking what you eat and drink each day. Hmm, that sounds a lot like the exercise you learned in chapter 7 for tracking your time and routines. Until you know what the issue is, you can't effectively begin to alter it.

So it is with the cause and effect of your life, and you don't often see it that clearly. It is easy for you to see how other demands on your time get in the way, but it is difficult to see how *you* get in the way.

ENLISTING THE HELP OF THE UNIVERSE

There is a whole universe out there that becomes a willing resource as soon as you open up to it. Writing your wishes as accomplishments gives you the space to choose how to fulfill them. Once you decide what your life is going to look like, you become more aware of opportunities as they present themselves to you.

When you write your accomplishments, you broadcast your wishes to the universe, and you raise your antenna to receive the answers. And, in your heightened state of receptivity, you will find that you attract precisely the answers you seek. You might be engaged in a conversation with a stranger who starts discussing the topic you were thinking about that morning. You become a magnet for those things that will fulfill your accomplishments.

REVIEWING YOUR ANNUAL ACCOMPLISHMENTS WEEKLY

You created your future when you wrote your annual accomplishments. You looked out a year ahead, created a list of what you will have accomplished during this year, and envisioned what life will be like then. In that moment, you were living into the future. Now, during your weekly review and planning time, go back to your future (your accomplishments) and again envision what life will be like for you a year from now. From this place, choose which areas you want to have an impact on this week.

Some people like to look at their accomplishments once a month, some once a quarter. When you first start, we encourage you to look at them at least every week. Eventually, you will discover a frequency that works for you. Each time you review your accomplishments, you can ask yourself, "Is this what I truly want?" If the answer is still "yes," this is the time to review your progress and see what structures and resources you need to set up to achieve your goals.

Next, go to your annual accomplishments list and look at the items you have written in that category and choose what you will schedule in your calendar. You have now created your week from your future. Why do we make such a point of this? After all, you are only scheduling, right? What we want to impress on you is that you do have a choice over how your days are designed.

Designing your days and weeks from the future you've created for yourself is a powerful practice. Writing out "how it's going to be" when you meet yourself at the end of the year provides you with the space and time to create your year and have it happen. Will you complete everything that you set out to complete this week? You probably won't, since you aren't practiced yet at understanding how long it takes you to complete tasks. But you do have the opportunity. If, however, you do not make the effort to design your days and weeks, you ensure that you will not accomplish what you want.

When you take the time to choose what you are going to do, and set yourself up to make it possible, you have a much better chance of staying present in the moment, instead of merely reacting when you're faced with interruptions, distractions, emergencies (perceived or real), and all the rest that the world throws at you. It is these few seconds, when you make choices about how your days are designed, that put you in control and keep you from being swept along by life.

WALL OF NO'S

Elizabeth Gilbert, author of the best-selling book *Eat, Pray, Love,* mentioned in an interview on *The Oprah Winfrey Show* a strategy for having focus in her life. She talked about surrounding herself with a "wall of no's" so that she could deliver on what she was saying yes to. For many women (and men), it is tempting to crowd our lives with yeses, and not designate time for ourselves and for the true priorities in our lives. There is great power that comes from being able to say "no."

A business's strategic plan helps its leaders decide not only what to do, but also what *not* to do. In creating a strategic plan for your life, it is equally important to identify what you are going to say "yes" to and what you are going to say "no" to. The clearer you are about how your time is being spent, and the more you fill your days with what you say is most important, the easier it is to say "no."

The Fine Art of Saying No

One of the great arts in life is learning how to say "no" in service to a higher "yes." Sometimes we see our task as "telling them no in such a way that they aren't upset and they still like me." But this is an almost impossible task because, if you are trying to manage another person's reaction, you may end up losing sight of what's important to you. Furthermore, you are trying to control something over which you have no control. So instead, as William Ury states in *The Power of a Positive No,* see your task as, "I need to tell them no in a way that is clear, honest, and respectful, and then let them react however they react."[1]

Listed here are some specific keywords or phrases you can use in saying no to other people's requests in a way that is authentic. Your tone and underlying intent need to be congruent with your words to have a positive impact.

- No, thank you.
- Thank you for the gracious invitation. I regret that I must decline.
- That sounds like a lot of fun, which makes it even harder for me to decline.
- I'm not able to do that right now.
- It is no for now.
- I have another commitment at that time.
- I'm sorry, I have plans that night. Thank you.
- I have an important family commitment.
- I'd rather decline than do a mediocre job.
- I'd like to help out; it's that I have other projects I am committed to finishing before I take on anything else.
- I'm sorry; I really can't give that project the attention it deserves.
- I'd love to help, but I'm on a strict deadline for the next few days. Let me know if there's any way I can help another time.
- Thank you. This really isn't my strong suit. Let me connect you with someone who can do it.
- Some things have come up that need my attention.
- No, I won't be able to make it, and please let me know how it goes.
- I'm sorry, as a general rule I don't participate in [insert activity here]. If there's another way I can help, let me know.

- I have a policy of [insert policy]. Example: "I have a policy of not gossiping."
- I can't right now, but I can do it [insert a specific time here].
- Unfortunately, I have other commitments right now. If you'd like, I can get back with you at [insert a specific time here].
- I can't right now, and I know you will do a wonderful job yourself.

What can you say no to that can give rise to a higher yes? Try this exercise: Think of one to two people you have a hard time saying no to, or you feel you can't say no to. Write down three to five different ways you can say no to them. Use the blank form in table 8-2.

The assumption we are making is that you want more time for you so that you can do what you want, when you want, and how you want more often. Right? Our signature motto is "create your life and design your days." If you want to have more time to do what your heart desires, then it will be critical for you to actively participate in designing and planning your life.

Your dreams can come true. In our mind, there is no question about that. But make no mistake: Dreams won't come true by wishing, hoping, thinking, wondering, or pleading. Dreams come true by being intentional, purposeful, grateful, and open, then taking committed, directed action toward the desired outcome. In this chapter, you learned how to keep the dreams of what you want to accomplish in front of you by reviewing your annual accomplishments and ensuring that every week you schedule time in your calendar to take action toward your dreams. The beauty of this process is that you'll begin to see your dreams unfold and come true in your life right before your eyes. You won't have to take our word on this

Table 8-2. Ways to say no.

NAME	HOW TO SAY NO

one, because "seeing is believing," and if you take on these practices, you're destined to become a believer. Dreams do come true when you plan.

In the following chapters, our attention turns to how to manage the daily deluge of electronic data. You'll learn a technique for handling e-mail and social media so that you can be in control and get things done.

9

MANAGING E-MAIL

The life we want is not merely the one we have chosen and
made. It is the one we must be choosing and making.
                                        —WENDELL BERRY

E-mail is a fairly recent phenomenon without a direct comparison. Unlike voice mail, it is visual; yet, unlike a letter, which is visual, there is no physical manifestation. It exists, but only in a box, and when you turn off the box, it doesn't exist anymore. We can ignore it.

Think about it. E-mail doesn't inhabit a physical space, but we like to say it takes up psychic space—it clutters your mind. It would be difficult to store thousands and thousands of files in our cubicles, yet we can store massive quantities of e-mail in our computer inboxes. And although there are fewer space constraints in the cyber world, we are affected as much by cyber clutter as we are by physical clutter. When the subject line is no longer bold, indicating that we have at least glanced at the e-mail, we skip over it easily. Yet it still sits there and is met by tens, hundreds, or even thousands of other messages, adding to the mountain of things we have to do and perpetuating our state of overwhelm.

It is time to let go of this habit of letting e-mail messages sit idle in your inbox. This chapter instructs you on how to keep your inbox empty. An empty inbox is a clear space that allows you to function optimally and takes away the dread of looking at your e-mail to begin with.

THE ELECTRONIC TYRANT

In the early 1990s, when e-mail first began gaining popularity, it was exciting to receive messages from other people and fun to write them back, knowing that our replies would reach them instantly. At some point, e-mail shifted from being a new way of communicating to being an automated work assigner. It became the way people would give us our daily tasks. Soon, our bosses and coworkers were sending us messages such as, "I need the changes to these documents right away," "Where is my report?" and "You didn't get back to my previous e-mail message." E-mail became a little dictator.

Now, the first thing people do when they arrive at work is read their e-mail messages. We all knew from the start that e-mail was meant to be a communication mechanism, but we didn't think it would become another demanding part of our job. Many people now use e-mail to structure their workday, even though they already know what their job is. They know their role in the company and understand what their department does. Yet they still go to their inbox to see what there is to do.

People are loyal to their e-mail. There appears to be an unwritten expectation that you are accessible and available, so if someone sends you something, you will read it, understand it, and respond immediately. That's the deal. And when you break the deal, you are not a team player, you are not on top of things, you are not competent, and something is wrong with you. Every day, and sometimes constantly throughout the day, you have to check your e-mail because there could be something there that, if left unopened, will have an impact on how you are perceived.

E-mail has become an electronic tyrant. It says, "Read me, feed me, do what I say." It demands our attention, directs our work, and has a controlling presence in our lives.

THE EVOLUTION OF BEING OVERWHELMED

It is not the volume of the e-mail that is the main issue causing the experience of feeling overwhelmed; it is our relationship to our e-mail that has generated a mountain of cyber clutter.

Before e-mail at work, there was interoffice mail. Most people did not have an issue with interoffice mail because it arrived in a stream, not a flood, and people did not let it pile up the way they do with e-mail. Also, at one time many people had office assistants who would handle their correspondence and sort out what was relevant.

When e-mail came along, businesses immediately recognized that it was a way for them to eliminate some of the paper clutter of interoffice mail and reduce the number of administrative assistants needed in the company. Most employees could handle their own communications and be their own administrative assistants.

It used to be that the only individuals with computers and access to e-mail were businesspeople. Before the e-mail boom, people in high-tech companies might receive twenty e-mails a day, but these were interoffice e-mails and could be dealt with in a workday. Now, everyone and their grandmother has an e-mail account, and all these people are sending us messages, whether we want them or not. E-mail usage has exploded, and we are not keeping up with its rate of expansion. The work practices that we developed ten, twenty, or thirty years ago are not sufficient to deal with the volume of e-mail received daily, and many of us are overwhelmed at the thought of checking our inbox. There are great costs associated with this wondrous technology of real-time communication.

MADISON AVENUE WANTS YOU

There are numerous studies, software programs, and analytic tools that report on how we read or don't read e-mailed advertising messages. An entirely new vocabulary has been established to define what we click through to, what we "hit," and what we do or don't do with any given message sent to us. There's even a science concerning when to send messages for the best chance of a response.

Seminars are available to train marketers in the psychology of how we behave when we view or don't view their messages and what they can do to improve their chances that we will take some action. According to Donovan Panone, vice president of online behavior at the interactive advertising agency Spunlogic, sellers "have about two to ten seconds to capture users' attention and persuade them to take action."[1] These marketers are learning to:

- Understand the psychological process that takes place when you receive their e-mail.
- Capitalize on the psychological factors of your intentions, motivations, and obstacles.
- Choose e-mail tactics as they relate to different stages of the buying process.

There is also a huge market for selling data about us to advertisers who can flood our inboxes with spam (unsolicited advertising messages). It has become so intense that we now purchase spam-blocking software in an attempt to keep these messages (and companies) away from our inboxes.

Madison Avenue wants you! And it's spending millions of dollars to keep you in its sights. Advertisers are coming after you, and they're getting better at honing in on how to get you to act when they send you e-mail. This contributes to the explosion of the number of messages in your inbox, and adds to your sense of it all being too much.

And you thought it was just *your* inbox that's out of control. So far we've only accounted for companies and organizations from the outside world that are cluttering up inboxes everywhere. We also have those inside our realm of influence: friends, family members, coworkers, and colleagues, such as members of organizations that we support, and so on. It's common now for people to receive hundreds of e-mail messages in a single day.

SINKING IN OUR PRIVATE SHAME

For many of us, there is a private shame associated with not responding to e-mail messages in a timely fashion and not managing our inbox, leaving hundreds if not thousands of e-mails lying in wait. No one else knows (other than your system administrator perhaps) how many messages are residing in your inbox. So you are alone in your private state of shame. You are hiding, and don't want anybody to know that your inbox is overflowing and out of control; you think you should know how to handle the volume, but you don't, and every day the e-mails keep mounting.

It's not hopeless, because the key to managing your inbox is having a reliable system and using it consistently. Later in this chapter we outline a step-by-step process for handling the ever-increasing volume of incoming e-mails and for maintaining an empty inbox.

THE CONSEQUENCES OF NOT DECIDING

Podiatrists get a lot of business from people with foot pain, and sometimes their patients are convinced they need surgery to alleviate the problem. You might be surprised that podiatrists often make this diagnosis: "You don't have a foot problem. You have a shoe problem. If you change the type of shoes you wear, you'll eliminate the pain."

Similarly, we don't have an e-mail problem; we have a decision-making problem. The volume of our e-mail is not the issue. It is our habit of not deciding to tackle the problem and believing that there are no consequences to our indecision.

There are consequences to not deciding. When the volume of e-mail builds we may feel that we will never be able to get our arms around all we have to do and handle. We feel guilty because we meant to get back to someone who e-mailed us, and now we haven't responded to that three-month-old message. We feel inadequate because everyone else seems to be able to handle their e-mail and we're the only ones having an issue. We feel that we are not good enough, not strong enough, and not smart enough, because good, strong, and smart people wouldn't have these problems with something as simple as e-mail. The consequences to not deciding are worry and self-loathing: worry because we are afraid that we will forget something; and self-loathing because we feel incompetent doing our jobs.

Our families bear the lingering effect of our not deciding. When we come home from work after a long day, we are distracted by the laundry list of things that we didn't finish. We are still thinking about an e-mail we forgot to send when, all of a sudden, one of our children comes up to us with pride and says that the teacher read their story in front of the class and we don't even hear it. We're still back in the office, lost in our list of everything we haven't done.

There are consequences that we may not be consciously aware of as it relates to our e-mail management habits. Our sense of peace of mind and well-being erodes when we are constantly concerned about reading and responding to e-mail messages.

It can be a particularly harrowing experience when we have not been able to check our e-mail for a few days. We open our inbox and are inundated with new messages. These e-mails are like incoming missiles. We want to take cover, we want to run, and we want to hide, but we have to deal with them.

THREE MOST COMMON E-MAIL PROBLEMS

We often hold on to our e-mails, secretly hoping that we will be able to read and respond to them all someday. The simple fact is that hardly anyone will ever read and respond to each and every e-mail in their inbox. Once we accept this fact, we can get a handle on our e-mail and keep it from controlling us. Let's explore three predominant problems that make handling e-mail challenging.

Problem 1: Many E-Mails Are Not Targeted to Us

Telemarketing used to be a major problem. Companies would call us day and night, interrupting dinner or waking us from a weekend nap. Then the National Do Not Call Registry was established, which allows us to block most telemarketers. So now the majority of people who call us, approximately 80 percent, are people that we need or wish to talk to. They have something to share, discuss, or set up with us. Most phone calls and voice messages are specifically intended for us.

Unlike the personal messages we receive by telephone, many of the messages that enter our inbox are not directed at us. They might be messages that we are copied on, newsletter subscriptions or distribution lists that no longer interest us, or messages that have slipped through the spam filter.

Problem 2: There's No Structure to Manage the Volume of Our E-Mail

How many people do you know who have more than 100 saved voice mail messages? Not one, right? Our phone service won't allow us to save more than about twenty messages. There is a structure in place for controlling the habit of letting our volume of messages get out of hand.

With e-mail, however, there are few limits to how many messages we can save. Even when your system manager limits the size of your inbox, you are able to save several thousand messages.

We are in uncharted territory in terms of the volume of the e-mail we can hold on to. And without structures in place, we allow ourselves to engage in flights of fancy about what we can keep there: "Oh, I might want to go to Kuala Lumpur someday," or "That conference sounds so great," or "I should read that book when I have the time." We keep these messages hanging around for weeks, months, and even years with the fantasy that we might need them someday. We have no agreement with ourselves about how to manage this barrage that comes into our personal inbox, and so we maintain the flood of 100, 500, even 5,000 e-mails that we may never read again after first opening them.

Problem 3: We Are Addicted to Our E-Mail

Many people are addicted to e-mail. If they are not monitoring their messages constantly, they become noticeably uncomfortable. We strongly encourage that you allow yourself only a specific number of times each day to handle your e-mail and that you schedule those times in your calendar. For some people, this is an unreasonable suggestion. The urge to check messages is too strong. The temptation to be browsing our inboxes is too great. We need to get a fix, so to speak. Somehow, we believe that there is something so fabulous (or so terrible) entering our inboxes that we stop everything and jump in and read the message.

Think about this: There you are, engaged in a phone call with a client, yet as soon as you hear the ding, "You've got mail," or see you have a new message on your screen, you go to your inbox and you scan the message. Why would you distract yourself with a message that might be spam while you are engaged in a discussion with a client?

One of our clients complained over and over again that his manager checked e-mail and answered his telephone during their scheduled meetings. It bothered him so much that he resorted to scheduling their meetings in a conference room or anywhere but his manager's office.

You hear the tapping of keyboards during conference calls; you see a cell phone perched above the steering wheel in the car next to you on the expressway; you pin on your badge of honor for responding at 2:00 a.m. And you say this is not an addiction?

Lisa, a participant in one of our workshops, was convinced that she could not change her habits. She had to check her e-mail every ten or fifteen minutes because she was in HR. And HR needs to be responsive to people: "H stands for human and R for resources," she explained with emphasis.

Having committed to give it a try, she shared with us what had happened since she changed her e-mail practices: "For the first time, I am getting out of work on time. I don't need to stay evenings to get reports written; now, I can do them during the day." She let everybody in her department know that she looks at her e-mail every two hours. For her, learning to manage her e-mail was the most insightful part of the whole workshop. It is the practice that has helped her regain some control over her day. She loved her job but it was consuming her life, and changing her habits around e-mail gave her control.

THE SECRET TO MANAGING E-MAIL IS TRIAGE

In chapter 6 we learned how to empty our capture tool daily using a triage method, the same process used by emergency room personnel, surgeons, nurses, and other caretakers who are trained and practiced in how to deal with an onslaught of emergencies, making quick decisions about what gets handled first, second, and third. The dictionary definition of the verb "to triage" has evolved to mean "order things by rank or importance." We are recommending that you apply the principles of triage to your e-mail as well.

Of all the new practices in this book, learning to triage e-mail often makes the biggest impact in people's lives. Imagine this scenario: You open your inbox in the morning and there are several new messages that want your attention. Because you now know how to triage (sort and handle) your messages, by midafternoon your inbox is empty. That's right, *empty*! All of your messages have been dealt with. I know, it sounds impossible, yet when you make simple choices about your inbox, this can be the world in which you live. These are not choices of complexity; they are choices of consistency.

CONTROLLING YOUR E-MAIL IN THREE STEPS

How do you tame your inbox? Here are some practical steps for managing your e-mail:

- Separate the facts from the feelings.
- Schedule e-mail handling time.
- Set up your e-mail triage folders.

The suggestions outlined here are based on implemention with Microsoft Outlook, the most popular e-mail product, but they can be adapted to most other e-mail applications.

STEP 1: SEPARATE THE FACTS FROM THE FEELINGS

Let's examine the volume of e-mail you receive and how you deal with it. First, assess your e-mail situation and how much of an intrusion it is in your life. You also want to look at your attitude toward e-mail. Then you need to reexamine these issues after you have changed your e-mail habits for a week, two weeks, and a month, so that you can gauge how your habits have changed. Why is this important? Because any personal practices (whether new or old) are only as strong as your understanding of the impact, the costs, and the commitment to a new way of life.

Assess Your E-Mail Volume and Handling Habits

Please write down your answer to each of the questions listed in tables 9-1 and 9-2. There are no right or wrong answers, and you may estimate. Assessing your current situation will allow you to compare your e-mail efficiency after you have implemented e-mail triage practices.

Assess How You Feel About E-Mail

Some people experience the constant barrage of e-mail as never-ending and overwhelming. For them it's burdensome to have to respond to each message immediately, whether or not they want to. But if they don't respond right away, as a consequence, they worry

Table 9-1. E-mail assessment, part 1.

E-MAIL ASSESSMENT	# OF E-MAILS
How many new e-mail messages do you receive in a day?	
How many times do you browse through your e-mails each day?	
How many "Already Read" messages are left in your inbox each night?	
How many "Unread" messages are left in your inbox each night?	
How much time do you spend on e-mail each day? _____ **# of hours**	

that the sender may think that they are lazy, uncaring, unreliable, not on top of things, or irresponsible. Other people have a different relationship to their e-mail. They look at their inbox and see it as a way of being and staying connected to others. For them, it isn't a burden at all to be in communication with other people. They are proud of their ability to be responsive and appreciate being a resource to others.

To change your habits around e-mail, it's important that you get in touch with the actual physical and emotional sensations that it invokes in you.

Also notice if your feelings about e-mail change, depending on your work setting and the day of the week. On Friday evening, you

Table 9-2. E-mail assessment, part 2.

E-MAIL ASSESSMENT	
How would you characterize your relationship with e-mail?	
What are your conditioned responses?	
How do you feel when you open your inbox?	

may be eager to clear out your inbox because you know that, come Monday, it will be full again. But coming back from a vacation, you may have a sinking feeling about opening your inbox, knowing that you will find hundreds of new messages to respond to. If you work in an environment where you are expected to respond immediately, you may feel anxious about making a mistake or sounding unimpressive.

STEP 2: SCHEDULE E-MAIL HANDLING TIME

Set aside specific times in your day for handling your e-mail messages—not browsing them, but handling them, which means either answering, deleting, or filing messages. The discipline is to avoid looking at your e-mail continuously during the day. We recommend that you set aside time each day (three to four periods of fifteen to thirty minutes each) that you designate for emptying your inbox. For example, most people find that thirty minutes first thing in the morning, then again in the midafternoon, and once more before leaving work or retiring for the evening works well. It allows you to stay on top of messages without being a slave to them.

For some of you, like Lisa in human resources, this is unthinkable, "What! I can't go that long without answering e-mail; my boss would have my head. I have clients to respond to."

If you have these concerns, one way to change is by retraining others. Yes, consider how you have taught your boss, clients, or coworkers that you are always sitting there waiting for an e-mail to come from them so you can pounce on it and respond. Now it's time to teach them something different. It will require that you talk with them about your new e-mail practices and how you will work with them. With your boss, you might use an adaptation of this example:

"Boss," you say, "you know how we've been asked to take on more assignments since the merger? Well, I've been looking at ways I can increase my capacity to be more effective. One of the areas I have identified is how much time I spend on e-mail each day. I'm in my inbox responding to messages every minute I'm not in a meeting. So, I'm establishing a routine where I set aside time in the morning, then around noon, and again at the end of the day to read and handle my e-mail. That will increase my available time for handling current and future projects. But that means a message that you send at, say, 9:00 a.m. won't be read or answered by me until noon. Of course, if it is something that needs immediate attention you can call me. Does that work for you?"

Setting up a procedure for calling someone if you need an answer urgently, in less than four hours, works well. It forces people out of their automatic habit of dashing off and sending another e-mail message. Ask yourself, "How critical is it that I get an answer in fewer than four hours?"

The goal is to increase your productivity by freeing up your day so that you are not just looking at your e-mail, but are handling it reliably three or four times a day. Figure 9-1 shows how to create appointments in your calendar for setting aside time first thing in the morning, during lunchtime, and at the end of the day.

"You mean I can only be on my BlackBerry three times a day?

Figure 9-1. Setting times to handle your e-mail.

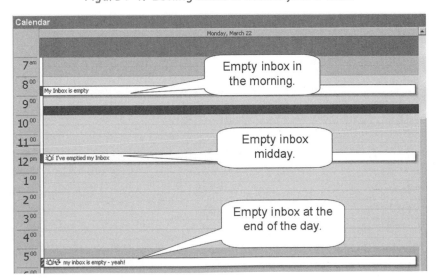

That's absurd!" Many people who use a smartphone find the idea of handling their e-mail messages only three, four, or five times a day difficult at first. They are currently tethered to their e-mail, checking it twenty, thirty, forty, or more times a day. If you travel, it may be appropriate to glance at your e-mail between appointments in order to stay on top of things. However, you still need to set aside adequate time to handle and respond to the messages and manage your e-mail to maintain an empty inbox. As you learn about e-mail triage, you may want to rethink the assumption that you always need to be available on a smartphone.

Setting aside specific times each day to read and handle your e-mail will add hours to your week. We waste so much time, more than we realize, browsing and rereading e-mail without answering it. Looking at the cyber clutter and the reminders of things we need to do but haven't done yet drains our energy and saps our creativity, often leaving us feeling rushed, unfocused, overwhelmed, and anxious.

Do it now. Open your calendar and create three reoccurring appointments every day during the week that you designate as time to handle—that is, read, respond, delete, or file—your e-mail. The best way to develop a new habit is to start now. So, yes, put down the book and create these appointments.

STEP 3: SET UP YOUR E-MAIL TRIAGE FOLDERS

The system that we offer is simple yet effective. It works well if you see it as a game of sorts. The goal is to keep your inbox empty. Yes, you read correctly—we said *empty*. You have already created three to four times each day to read, respond to, and handle your e-mail. That alone frees up valuable time for doing some of the important tasks that you might otherwise push aside because of a lack of time. To be able to continue this practice in the face of the ever-increasing volume of e-mail, we suggest learning to triage. This system works for people receiving as few as fifty and as many as 250 or more messages a day. It lets you choose *when* to handle and how to handle your messages.

A triage process gives you the peace of mind that comes from knowing that you will not forget or overlook an e-mail message that doesn't have top priority but is still important. You will save time by making decisions once, not repeatedly throughout the day.

Table 9-3 outlines the triage decision process for handling e-mails, describing the suggested folders you will set up and their

Table 9-3. E-mail triage process and decision tree.

Delete	Delete any messages you have handled or don't want or need to respond to.
Do It Now	Instantly answer anything that you can respond to in less than two minutes. Think of the Nike brand slogan: "Just do it."
Respond Today	You decide, "This message must be handled today. I'm going to need more than two minutes to respond." Drag it into your Respond Today e-mail folder. (Note: When you complete emptying your inbox, you dive right into this folder.)
Schedule a Specific Time in Your Calendar to Answer/Complete	"I need to do something about this. There is no way I'm going to complete it today. I need to pull some materials together. I will schedule one or more appointments in my calendar. It could take me an hour to respond."
Waiting for Response	For messages that you intend to respond to, but need information from someone else first, drag them to your Waiting for Response folder.
File It or Create a Folder	File it in an existing folder if it's important enough to file for future reference, or create a new folder for it.
Someday	"I'm not going to respond to this message, nor am I going to take the time to set up a file for it. However, I'd like to 'keep it around' just in case. I'll drag it to my Someday folder."
Freedom	For those of you who have a considerable number of read or unread messages in your inbox now, create a Freedom folder, which is where you can move all messages older than two days.

uses. In the same way you needed special folders to triage information recorded in your capture tool, you need new folders to triage your incoming e-mail.

Create New E-Mail Folders

To get started, let's create some folders (see figure 9-2). First, create an e-mail management folder. To keep it for easy access, label it #E-mail Management. You will notice that this file name appears at the top of your personal folder list, rather than buried in the midst of your folders. To handle the increased volume of e-mail, where we may get hundreds of messages per day (as compared to our capture tool, where we may record dozens of items per day), we'll make two new subfolders:

- Respond Today
- Freedom

Next, let's move some previously created folders into the #E-mail Management folder. They are:

Figure 9-2. Setting up your "Respond Today" and "Freedom"
e-mail management folders.

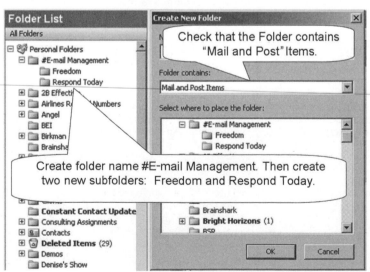

• Waiting for Response
• Someday

To move them, highlight the folder names in your personal folder list and drag them into #E-mail Management. Highlight the Waiting for Response folder, left-click, then drag it to the #E-mail Management folder (see figure 9-3). Repeat this process for the Someday folder. Now everything you need to triage your capture tool and e-mail is easily accessible. When done, your new #E-mail Management folders will look like the screen shown in figure 9-4.

With the e-mail triage folders and subfolders in place, you are ready to start practicing the e-mail triage process.

LEARNING THE TRIAGE PROCESS

Learning to triage e-mail often makes a big impact in people's lives. Here's how: You open your inbox in the morning and there are twenty new messages and several that need your attention right

Figure 9-3. Setting up your Waiting for Response
e-mail management folder.

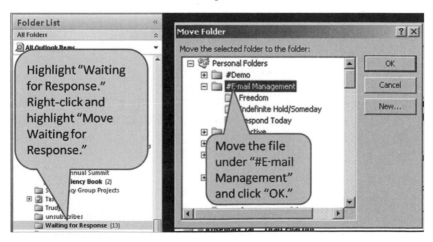

Figure 9-4. Completed setup of your e-mail management folders.

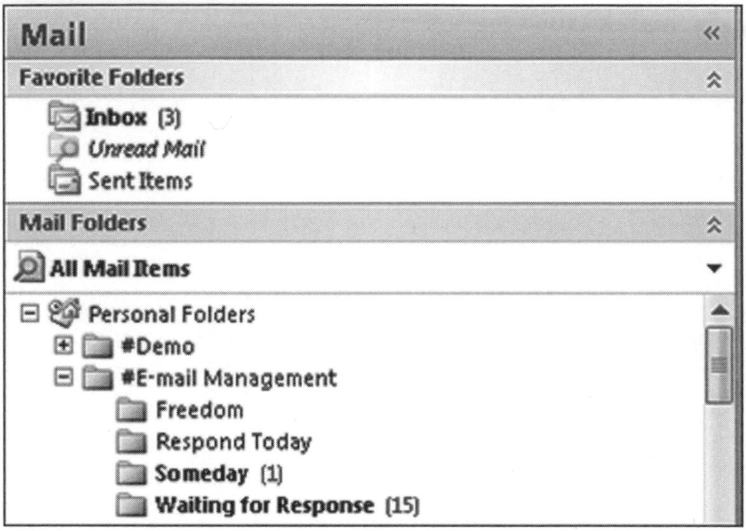

away. Because you now know how to triage, you Delete, Do, or File your messages, responding to the ones you choose to respond to now, leaving an empty inbox before your day even gets going.

You may notice how familiar the e-mail triage process is to the capture and release triage process covered in chapter 6. We have simply added two more folders for e-mail to handle the increased volume. Let's go through the e-mail triage decision tree, step by step.

Delete

Delete it. Delete, delete, delete. It's a beautiful thing. It's like a video game where you zap alien space invaders: Delete, delete, delete. Delete any messages you have already taken action on and completed, including any messages:

- You have read and have no further interest in.
- You have responded to.
- You don't need to read.

Do It

When you are handling items in your inbox during one of the designated times, respond right away to any messages that you can. Think of the Nike brand slogan: "Just do it." You have set aside this time to handle your e-mail, so touch it once and answer it. Here are the basics:

- Anything you can complete in under two minutes, just do it now.
- If you are committed to doing it today and it will take more than two minutes, drag it to your Respond Today folder. Once you have triaged your inbox to empty, you open this folder and begin responding.
- If you are committed to handling the e-mail but won't get to it today and need a substantial amount of time to think it through before responding, then drag it to your calendar, update the appointment form, and create time for it in your calendar.
- If you are committed to responding to the e-mail but can't because you need further information from someone else before you can do it, drag it to your Waiting for Response folder.

Respond Today

As you are answering and deleting messages, you will probably come upon one message where you think, "This must get handled today, but I need to think about it a little more," or "This message must be answered today, and it's going to take me five to ten minutes to write the response." Drag that e-mail into your Respond Today folder. You have another two to three times set aside before the day is over to empty your inbox and respond to your e-mail messages. At first you may feel this is creating extra work—moving the message to another folder. Or you may think, "I can't. I'll forget that it's there and needs to be answered." These are valid concerns when you are looking at the situation from your current method of operating. However, with your new system of setting aside three to four times each day to handle e-mails, you will have built in the time to handle all of the messages in your Respond Today folder. And, if you find you need more time, you can always increase the time you set aside.

Schedule a Specific Time to Answer in Your Calendar

As you are clearing out your inbox, invariably you'll encounter an e-mail where you say to yourself, "I need to do something about this but there is no way I can complete it today. As a matter of fact, I need some time to complete the request or assignment. In addition, I need to pull together some materials." For these types of issues that require time for making requests, doing research, creating content, or completing any series of actions, we recommend that you schedule specific sufficient time in your calendar to complete the work.

Drag It to Waiting for Response

When you are handling the messages in your inbox, you will likely run across a message that you want to be reminded of because it tells you that:

- The desired information will be forthcoming.
- Someone owes you certain information.
- There is something you want to do, but need further information first.

Rather than leave this message to clutter your inbox, drag it to your Waiting for Response folder. You can use this folder in the same way you use it to empty your capture tool, but instead of posting a note to the folder, since this is an e-mail message, simply drag the message into the folder. You do not need to be worried about forgetting these messages because reviewing this folder at least once a day is already a part of your daily effectiveness program.

File It

If it's something you want to save, place it in an existing file or create one.

If it's something you might want to save just because you never know if you'll need it, but you don't want to take the time to create a file for it, send it to your Someday folder.

Create Reference Folders

Consider, for example, the e-mail messages you receive that refer to a project you're interested in or may be working on, but require no response from you. If you want to keep them, create a project folder. Then drag the e-mail into that folder where you know it will be if you need to refer to it later.

File It in Your Someday Folder

Using your Someday Folder is a great way to take care of those messages pertaining to topics of interest, such as conferences you may want to attend, newsletters you may want to receive, ideas, and so forth. What they all have in common is 1) you are not going to do anything about this now, 2) it is not important enough for you to create a separate e-mail folder for, and 3) you're not ready to delete it entirely. You may think, "There'll be so much information in that file, how will I ever find anything?" Well, you will use whatever methods you are currently using for finding things in your overly full inbox, such as sorting by "Date," by "From," or by "Subject." Also, try downloading the Google Desktop tool (http://desktop.google.com). We've found that Google Desktop is a great way to search your own computer by typing in any term to find what you are looking for.

There's no need to schedule specific times in your calendar to review the items in your Someday folder. When that someday comes and you need to find something, it will be waiting for you right there in the folder.

Blind Copy to the Waiting for Response Folder

Previously, we introduced the Waiting for Response folder as part of your triage process to keep messages that you are waiting for

someone to respond to or waiting for someone to send you information about. There's another great way to use this folder. When
you are sending a message to someone requesting they do something for you, blind copy yourself on the message, and when it hits
your inbox, drag that message into this folder. The Bcc designation
doesn't always appear automatically on all e-mail forms, so you
have to go through a few steps to insert your name to receive a
blind copy. First, select "Cc" on the e-mail message you are creating
to open the "Select Names" dialog box (see figure 9-5).

In the Select Names dialog box, scroll until you find your name
and highlight it. Then click on "Bcc" at the bottom of the dialog
box. Your name should appear in the box next to "Bcc" (see figure
9-6). Then click OK.

Now your name will appear on the e-mail form (figure 9-7), but
will not appear to others who receive the e-mail.

When you are creating a message and you know that you want
a response from someone, that is the time to blind copy yourself. It
doesn't take more than an extra couple seconds and it sets in motion a process that provides you with the security of knowing that

Figure 9-5. Blind copy yourself, step 1.

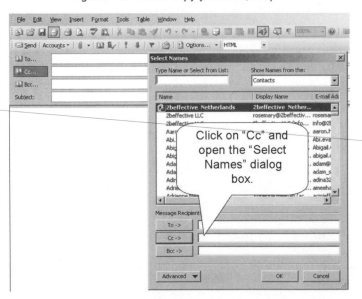

Figure 9-6. Blind copy yourself, step 2.

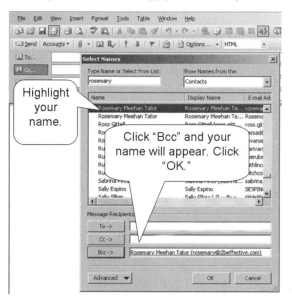

Figure 9-7. Blind copy yourself, step 3.

you have a reminder handy to see if the person got back to you. Creating a place where you can reliably be reminded that you need to receive a response from someone else has two benefits: You no longer have to worry about forgetting, and yet you keep the thought of these e-mails out of your mind right now, when you need to give attention to other matters.

We recommend that you make checking this folder part of your end-of-the-day routine. As you go through this folder and discover that many of the items may have already been handled—delete those messages. You may find that you are okay leaving some unattended for another day—leave them. You may find that some of them haven't been responded to and you need to take action. In this case, choose the appropriate action: e-mail, phone call, or stop by for a face-to-face meeting with the person.

Once you've established a Waiting for Response folder and the practice of checking it each day, there is another way this folder can be useful. If you are anxious about some people getting back to you with answers you need, why not use the Waiting for Response folder for another purpose: posting reminders for voice mail messages as well as e-mail when you want a response? When you are leaving a voice mail message and a response is needed, you can also post a note to your Waiting for Response folder. Then, when you check this folder at the end of the day, you can see every voice mail that you've left, as well as every e-mail, and you will know who has and hasn't responded to you. It is another load off your mind.

Achieve Freedom

Realizing that you may currently have hundreds or thousands of messages in your inbox, we created the concept of the Freedom folder as a place to hold all of that old e-mail. To begin, go into your inbox and move every message that's more than two days old into your new Freedom folder. Don't worry about moving them. You now know exactly where they are and can get to them anytime you want. You still have all the searching capabilities you had in your inbox.

The advantage is they are out of your inbox. We know that at first, this sounds like something way too risky to do. This is one of those times we say, "Just do it." Remember, you haven't "lost" any messages. They are no less important; they are just in the Freedom folder.

We recommend that you schedule a few times in your calendar this first week to review and handle the messages in your Freedom folder. Taking this step clears the way for you to actually tackle your inbox and manage it to zero. We promise: It works. Everyone we've advised and who has taken this step has told us how great they felt after they did it. You only need to use the Freedom folder this one time as a way to begin.

It can also be useful if sometime in the future you "fall off the wagon" and end up with hundreds of e-mail messages again. Simply move all items older than two days into your Freedom folder and you're back in control of your inbox.

STARTING ON YOUR WAY TO AN EMPTY INBOX

So now that your folders are set up and you understand the triage process, begin by moving all messages older than two days into your Freedom folder, and then continue to triage the remaining messages. Every time you open your inbox, your goal is to leave it empty. You will be making decisions constantly to do one of the following with each message:

- Delete it.
- Do it now.
- Respond to it today.
- Schedule a time in your calendar to answer or complete it.
- Drag it to the Waiting for Response folder.
- File it under Someday.
- File it in another folder you create.

Before the time allotted to handle your e-mail is up, your inbox is empty. Imagine that! Although your inbox continues to amass new messages, often at an alarming rate, you are not worried. You are cool, calm, and collected because there are other times in your day set aside to handle your e-mail.

Master Your E-Mail During the Day

Let's say that the next time set aside in your calendar to empty your inbox is around lunchtime. The first thing you do is open your inbox and repeat the triage process. You finish the triage process with time to spare. When this happens, go into your Respond Today folder and start responding to those messages. The alarm goes off, there is no more time left; it's time to go off to a meeting. That's okay because you know you are going to have more time during the day set aside for handling your e-mails.

You are becoming the master of your e-mails, instead of the other way around. You are choosing how and when you will handle them. You are touching each e-mail once; if you can handle it and do it, delete it and move it, you do it instantly. You are only moving the e-mails to another folder when you've made the choice of when and how you are going to address them. The psychic energy you get from an empty inbox is worth that extra step of placing each of those e-mail messages into another folder.

You have also chosen when you will respond to the e-mail. The reality is that you may not presently have the time to handle it, or you choose not to handle it at this moment, but you have designated a time in the future when it can be answered. There is peace of mind in knowing that you have a system in place that keeps you in control of what arrives in your inbox.

Clear Your Mind with an Empty Inbox

When you use the triage process to create an empty inbox, you gain a more finite view of what's important for the day and what's not. You have quantified what you need to get done and when you will do it. You are "up to the minute" on what's happening in your life and living in the moment when your inbox is cleared. It helps you strip away the sense of overwhelm.

You are in control of your day and your week because you are emptying your inbox. It's that basic.

10

REDUCING E-MAIL VOLUME

If a cluttered desk is the sign of a cluttered mind, what is the significance of a clean desk?

—DR. LAURENCE J. PETER

You can do a number of things to reduce the amount of e-mail you receive:

- Unsubscribe.
- Create a delete rule.
- Create rules for projects and people.
- Tell people you're making changes in your e-mail practices.

Taking the time to diminish the amount of incoming e-mail will have an immediate payoff. Try some of these methods to reduce the size of your inbox.

TIP 1: UNSUBSCRIBE

When you see an e-mail message in your inbox that you don't want to read or keep, take the thirty seconds it takes to unsubscribe. If you can't take those thirty seconds, create an "unsubscribe" folder and drag the message to that folder.

Then, once a month, set up a recurring 30-minute appointment to unsubscribe to all of the messages sitting in the "Unsubscribe" folder.

TIP 2: CREATE A DELETE RULE

For the other messages that you can't unsubscribe to easily and that keep coming, create an e-mail rule to automatically delete them. You can create a rule so that anytime you get an e-mail from "John Doe," that e-mail is automatically sent to your deleted messages folder.

It's not uncommon to receive information about products that you were once interested in or ordered online two years ago, but aren't anymore. These messages keep coming, and you can't unsubscribe because you no longer have the login information you need to unsubscribe. Don't waste any more time; create a rule. Send the message directly to your deleted items folder.

Let's create a delete rule for John Doe, someone who used to work with you but has moved on and keeps sending out e-mail blasts to a distribution list that has your name on it. He didn't respond to your request to delete your name. For this rule, we are going to instruct Microsoft Outlook to delete all e-mail coming from John Doe by placing it in the Delete folder.

First, make sure you have a contact record for the person whose messages you want to send directly to the Delete folder. If you don't know how to create a contact record, you can use the instructions Microsoft Outlook provides in the Help option.

Next, in the Microsoft Outlook toolbar, click on Tools to bring up a drop-down menu (as shown in figure 10-1). Click on "Rules and Alerts" to open the Rules and Alerts dialog box (figure 10-2). To create a rule for John Doe, click on the New Rule tab.

Clicking on the New Rule tab brings up the Rules Wizard dialog box. In the top section of this box labeled Step 1: Select a

Figure 10-1. Creating a delete rule, step 1.

Figure 10-2. Creating a delete rule, step 2.

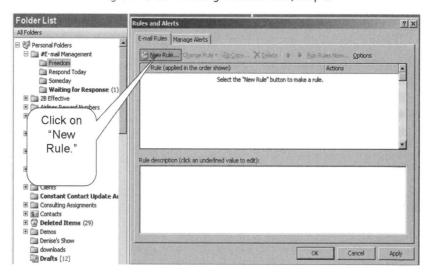

template, the first line in bold is "Stay Organized." Just below it, select "Move messages from someone to this folder" (see figure 10-3).

In the Rules Wizard dialog box, under the section labeled Step 2: Edit the rule description (click an underlined value), click on "people or distribution list." This action brings up the Rule Address dialog box. Enter the name you are creating the delete rule for— "John Doe," in our example. As you type, you'll see your contact list

Figure 10-3. Creating a delete rule to move messages to a folder.

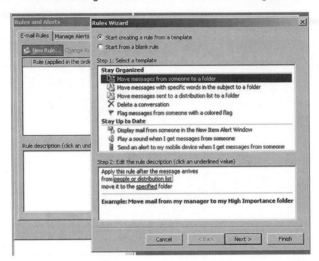

and the name highlighted and you can select the name from your address book, then click OK (see figure 10-4).

Selecting the name brings up the Rules Wizard dialog box once again. Only now, in the lower half of the dialog box, in the section labeled Step 2: Edit the rule description, you will see that the name John Doe and his e-mail address have replaced the "people or distribution list" selection. Just below, click on "specified" folder (see figure 10-5). This action brings up your Personal Folder List. Highlight "Deleted Items" and click OK (figure 10-6).

There are a few more steps to confirm the rule settings. When you click OK, the Rules Wizard menu reappears. Clicking on "Next" brings up a list of options in the top section of the dialog box (titled Step 1: Select a template). Make sure that the box next to "Move messages from someone to a folder" is checked and select it if it is not (see figure 10-7). Then click "Next."

Clicking on "Next" brings a new list of options in the Rules Wizard menu under Step 1: Select condition(s). Make sure that the box next to "from people or distribution list" is checked (see figure 10-8) and select it if it is not. Then click "Next."

Figure 10-4. Creating a delete rule by selecting names
from your contact list.

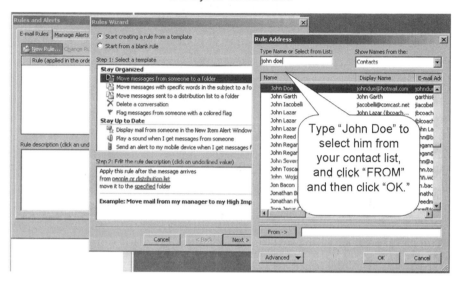

Figure 10-5. Creating a delete rule by specifying an
e-mail address and folder.

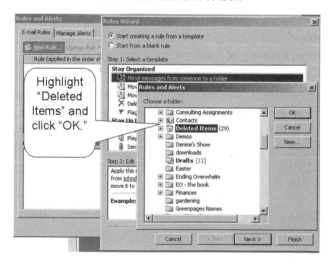

Figure 10-6. Confirming the rule settings, step 1.

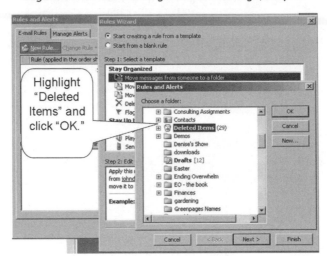

Figure 10-7. Confirming the rule settings, step 2.

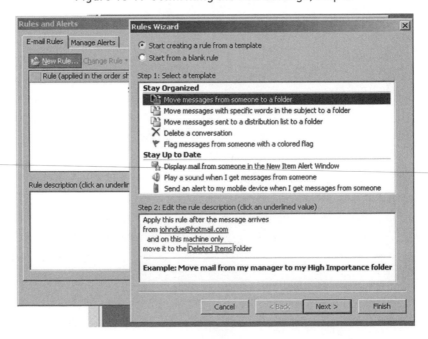

Figure 10-8. Confirming the rule settings by selecting the conditions.

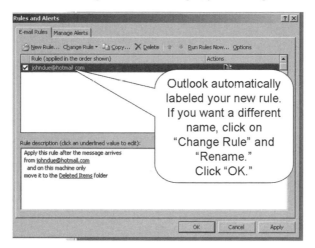

Once you click "Next," the next confirmation screen (figure 10-9) will show Step 1: Select action(s). Make sure "move to specified folder" is checked. Then select "Next."

The next Rules Wizard screen (figure 10-10) asks about encryption. There is no need for any encryption, so click "Next."

Next, the Rules Wizard lets you specify a name for the rule (see figure 10-11). The name and e-mail address you initially selected for this rule should appear in the selection box. If you want a different name for your rule, type it in now. Also, make sure the box is checked to "Turn on the rule." Click "Finish" and the rule goes into effect.

You now have a rule to ensure that messages from Joe Doe go directly to your Delete folder. Microsoft Outlook Help has instructions for how you can copy a rule and then modify it with other e-mail addresses that you want to send directly to your Delete folder, which simplifies the process of creating the rule. You can also copy a rule and then modify it for moving messages from your inbox to a specific folder. This feature is particularly useful for:

• Groups you belong to (sending all their messages to one folder)
• Distribution lists you are on (sending all of these messages to one folder)

Figure 10-9. Confirming the rule settings by selecting an action.

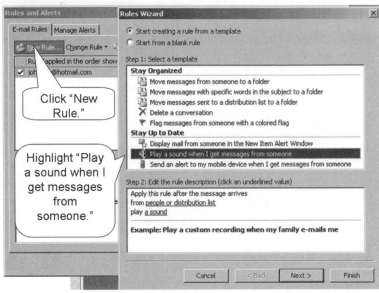

Figure 10-10. Selecting "no encryption" for the rule settings.

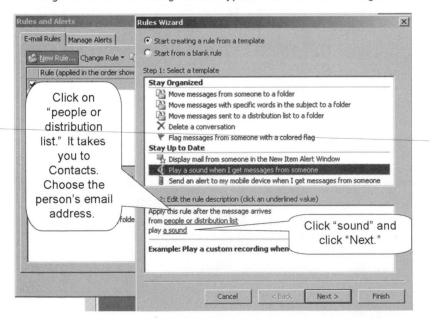

Figure10-11. Specifying a name for the delete rule.

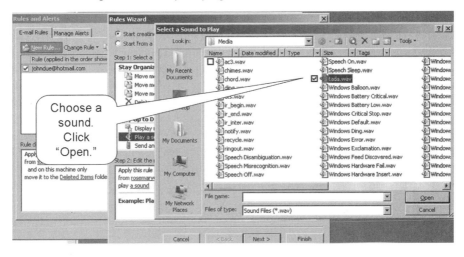

TIP 3: CREATE RULES FOR PROJECTS AND PEOPLE

For projects that you are working on, or for groups that you meet with regularly, set up a rule in your inbox to automatically send a copy of these e-mails to the folder for that project or group. (Instructions for creating this rule are described in Appendix B.) If you don't need to respond to the e-mail or take any other action when it arrives in your inbox, you can just delete it from your inbox because you know it's already copied in the appropriate project or group folder. This is useful for situations where you get a lot of messages and want to keep a record of communications from, for example:

- Project teams
- People in your work group
- Customers
- Your manager
- Your direct reports

See how quickly the triage can go in your inbox? You are able to immediately delete all those messages, knowing that they've already been appropriately stored.

TIP 4: CREATE RULES AS ALERTS FOR MESSAGES FROM CERTAIN PEOPLE

By now you are viewing your e-mail messages only three to five times per day, during the times set in your calendar. But sometimes you may be working with a client who has particular concerns that are time critical, or you may be waiting for some important information from your spouse or daughter and you want to know it has arrived in your inbox without having to constantly monitor your e-mails. For these situations a useful feature is to create an Alert. An alert is a specific sound for that person. The alert can be used just for a day or, in the case of some of your work clients, longer.

Creating an alert is very similar to creating rules. Now that you are familiar with the process of creating rules in Microsoft Outlook (as illustrated in figures 10-1 through 10-11), let's just walk through the steps for creating an alert:

1. In the Outlook toolbar, select Tools. From the drop-down menu, highlight "New Rule." It brings up the "Rules and Alerts" dialog box.

2. Click "New Rule" to bring up the "Rules Wizard" dialog box.

3. In the dialog box, under Step 1: Select a template, go to the list item called "Stay Up to Date" and click on "Play a sound when I get a message from someone."

4. In the Rules Wizard dialog box, under Step 2: Edit the rule description (click an underlined value), click on "people or distribution list."

5. Choose the person or distribution list and click "OK."

6. Under Step 2: Edit the rule description, this time click on "play a sound."

7. Choose a sound and click "OK."

8. Continue through the rules setting sequence by clicking "Next" and naming the rule, then click "Finish."

Figure 10-12 shows the screen you will see after setting up this rule. Notice the sound icon.

TIP 5: TELL PEOPLE YOU ARE MAKING CHANGES IN YOUR E-MAIL PRACTICES

Unless you are someone who likes to receive joke e-mails if only for the joy of deleting them, tell people who are sending them to stop because, as part of the changes you are making to be more effective

Figure10-12. Creating a sound alert for an incoming message.

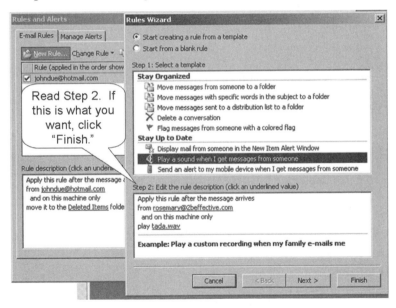

this year, you are striving to reduce the number of e-mails you need to process.

Let people know that, unless there is something they think you must look at, don't send it. You can ask people to delete you from their distribution lists, especially when it comes to chain letters or jokes.

If you are being automatically CC'd by someone unnecessarily, ask to be taken off of the list.

TIP 6: ASK PEOPLE TO THINK BEFORE PRESSING "REPLY TO ALL"

Remind people who have the tendency to automatically press "Reply to All" to ask whether the intended recipients all need to read what they're sending. Is it going to enhance their day or are they cluttering up someone else's e-mail? Just because we are not paying postage for each message going out on the Internet doesn't mean that we are not paying a cost of some sort—we are all, every one of us, paying with our time.

There are many tactics you can implement to reduce the volume of e-mail you receive. Remember to unsubscribe to anything that is just taking up psychic RAM. When you can't unsubscribe, set up a delete rule. For frequently recurring e-mail, set up rules to handle it automatically so that you no longer need to move it into folders. Let your colleagues, coworkers, family members, and friends know that you are making changes in your e-mail practices and ask for their help. Remind those people around you who frequently use "Reply to All" to think about whether their e-mail responses are relevant to everyone on the list.

11

BACK ON THE TRIAGE WAGON

It's at the end of the day and there are an additional thirty unanswered messages in your inbox and sixteen messages to answer in the Respond Today folder. There will be times when you fall behind in triaging your e-mail. Don't panic. All you need to do is create a weekly stopgap time where you empty your inbox and get caught up. This practice gives you a fresh start each week and sets you up to be the master of your inbox rather than the victim of it.

If you have e-mail messages that have been sitting in your inbox for a week or two and you aren't doing anything about them, you might as well move them to your Someday folder. That way if you need them, you can easily find them there. It's not bogging you down—you are making a choice about how you are handling it.

Remember, when you put e-mail in the Someday folder, you are not sending it to Siberia. You still have access to those messages whenever you like. Keep your inbox empty. Clean out your Respond Today folder every day. Make it a practice.

It's like housework. Sometimes you spit-shine the floor and it's gorgeous—the floor gleams when the sun shines in on it and you demand everyone be careful about not wearing shoes in the house. And then life hits. Milk spills. The dog tracks mud in and you've got to clean it again. But you don't have the time at the moment to tackle it with a spit-shine, so for now just sweeping will do. Eventually, however, the floor will get so dirty that you'll surrender and say, "That's enough already. I'm scrubbing the floor again."

It's not that different with your e-mail. It's maintenance. Having a set routine for handling your e-mail messages will keep you on track.

E-MAIL IS ONLY *ONE* COMMUNICATION VEHICLE

There are many communication vehicles at our disposal, including face-to-face communication, the telephone, leaving voice mail messages, sending snail or express mail, text messaging, instant messaging (IM), tweeting, and faxing. And then there is e-mail, which is often the vehicle of choice because it is quick, easy, and free. It has become the preferred method of communication for many people.

E-mail is great for transactional correspondence, but there are times when the message you are sending is too critical or sensitive to be sent via e-mail. It breaks down when you want to convey emotion or when the message is more complex. When you need to reply to a message and ask for clarification, it is okay if you have one question. More than one and you should ask whether a phone call would be more expedient. When a message becomes more complex and nuanced, the human voice becomes the most effective vehicle to transmit both its emotional meaning and its content. Talking an issue through is much faster than e-mailing, even if you use IM, because there is so much information you hear in the tonality of the voice that can't be conveyed with text.

An e-mail sent does not equal a communication received. There is a difference between sending a message and the act of communicating. Often we think we've communicated, but all we've done is written and distributed electronic data. You've communicated only when you have checked in with the receiver(s) of the message and confirmed that you both have the same understanding of the message.

Opportunities for Miscommunication

Psychologists Justin Kruger and Nicholas Epley of the University of Chicago have published research that helps explain why these electronic misunderstandings occur so frequently.[1] They find that when people send e-mail, they overestimate both their ability to convey their intended tone—be it sarcastic, serious, or funny—as well as their ability to correctly interpret the tone of messages that others send to them.

The reason for this communication disconnect, the researchers find, is egocentrism—the well-established social psychological phenomenon whereby people have a difficult time detaching themselves from their own perspectives and understanding how other people will interpret them. And as e-mail has become more prevalent, Epley says, the opportunities for misunderstanding have increased. "Of course there's nothing new about text-based communication; people have been writing letters for centuries," he explains. "But what's different in this medium is . . . the ease with which we can fire things back and forth. It makes text-based communication seem more informal and more like face-to-face communication than it is."

Despite this ease, though, e-mail can have some serious disadvantages. In their study, Kruger and Epley found that people are better at communicating and interpreting tone in vocal messages than in text-based ones. "I think people do have some intuition, abstractly, about the limits of e-mail," Epley says. "But I don't think that in specific instances people realize that a *particular* message is unclear."

Given these findings, then, what's the average e-mailer to do? Well, perhaps pick up the phone. "E-mail is fine if you just want to communicate content, but not any emotional material," Epley explains.

Think About the Receiver

Just as we encourage you to ask others to be mindful of their e-mail practices, you need to think about the receiver before you send an e-mail message. Every time you click "Reply to All," you are adding to the volume of other people's inboxes. Every time you get that great inspirational quote, or that joke that had you laughing your socks off, and you sent it out, you are cluttering up someone else's e-mail. Think before sending.

CURBING THE SENSE OF BEING OVERWHELMED

The most common and vocal complaint we hear around productivity and effectiveness is "I'm being overwhelmed by my e-mail." Client after client, workshop after workshop, it is the biggest issue that people face. E-mail contributes to their sense of being overwhelmed.

We are not saying you will never feel overwhelmed again because your inbox is empty. We're saying that reducing the number of e-mails that have taken permanent residency in your inbox will eliminate a significant source of stress. Handle your e-mail and you will start developing the muscle that it takes to handle the rest of your life.

Every day when you look at your empty inbox, you are going to say to yourself, "I did it. I conquered the e-mail tyrant." And you'll feel energized, which is how you need to feel if you want to have a rich, rewarding, fulfilling, satisfying life. The next chapter will give you a similar process for handling social media.

12

SOCIAL MEDIA IS
HERE TO STAY

Is social media a fad or the biggest shift since the Industrial Revolution?

—ERIK QUALMAN

Social media is a global phenomenon. The usage statistics are staggering. According to Nielsen Online's 2009 analysis of social media marketing, social networks and blogs beat other online activity, including personal e-mail, to become the most popular online activity.[1]

Using social media is a new way of communicating that can foster community and collaboration. It is literally six degrees of separation in action. You can make connections with new professionals, old colleagues, suppliers, and customers in minutes and never have to leave the comfort of your home or workplace to do so. There are numerous social media outlets that are revolutionizing the way we conduct our personal and business lives. The three most popular social media destinations are Facebook, LinkedIn, and Twitter.

Although social media offers huge advantages to the way we live and work, a potential adverse side effect is that a significant number of hours can be whittled away engaging in these sites. This chapter is about how to manage the social media that you use now or may use in the future. It is not our intent to describe the benefits of one form of social media over another. Rather, we want to outline a process to manage your time using these social media sites so that they add value to your life and do not become a distraction or burden.

WHAT CURRENT SITES OFFER

Let's begin by exploring what each of the most popular social media sites have to offer. Here is a cursory overview.

LinkedIn

LinkedIn (www.linkedin.com) is currently the largest business and professional network where people exchange information and ideas. More than 50 million professionals worldwide use LinkedIn to find and introduce themselves to potential clients, service providers, and subject matter experts who come recommended; to find business opportunities; to discover inside connections that can help land a job; and to get advice from trusted professionals.

Facebook

With more than 400 million users, Facebook (www.facebook.com) is arguably the largest social network as of this writing. Originally designed as a network for college students, Facebook is now used by individuals, businesses, and families around the world to stay connected with people in their lives. Facebook's mission is to "give people the power to share and make the world more open and connected." People use Facebook every day to upload an unlimited number of photos, share links and videos, and learn more about the people they meet. Facebook has been banned by some employers to discourage their employees from wasting time. Nevertheless, its growth continues and its fastest-growing user segment is 35-year-olds and older.

Twitter

Twitter (www.twitter.com) is a social networking and microblogging service that allows you to answer the question "What are you doing?" with short text messages called "tweets." You sent tweets to your friends, or "followers," via mobile texting, IM, or the Web. Twitter was designed to let people "share and discover what's happening right now, anywhere in the world." The short format of the tweet (140 characters in length) is a defining characteristic of the service, allowing informal collaboration and quick information sharing that provides relief from rising e-mail and IM fatigue. You can share information with people you wouldn't normally exchange e-mail or IM messages with, opening up your circle of contacts to an ever-growing community of like-minded people.

These technologies are becoming a mainstay in business. Social media outlets are used to research information about prospects before engaging with them, to survey customers to see how we can serve them better, to find new employees, and to stay on top of marketplace trends. Personal lives are also benefiting. Social media has made it much easier to get reacquainted with people from our past and to keep in contact with new friends. In fact, one out of eight couples married in the United States in 2008 met online.[2]

MANAGING OUR SOCIAL MEDIA USAGE

Although these social media outlets offer many benefits, they can also consume enormous amounts of time. It takes time to answer invitations and questions from colleagues on LinkedIn, and to answer friends and post and update your pages in Facebook, and to add followers and answer direct tweets on Twitter. Just as e-mail can be an all-consuming function that you must learn how to manage (as covered in chapter 9), it is equally important to become strategic about your social media usage so that you can benefit from its many advantages. When it comes to effectively managing social media, the key decisions are:

- Why you are using it?
- What do you want to accomplish?
- How important is it?
- How much time are you willing to devote?

Step 1: Determine Why and How You Are Using Social Media

Use table 12-1 to identify why you use social media and then which sites you frequent. As an example, a common business reason for using social media is to learn more about prospects. Let's say that you currently use both Facebook and LinkedIn to routinely learn more about possible clients, so place an X in the boxes to the right of that line in the table. You can customize this chart, adding other uses and other sites, to reflect you own preferences.

Step 2: Determine What You Want to Accomplish

Now that we know how and why you are using these various services, let's look at what you want to accomplish by using them. Just

Table 12-1. Why and how you are using social media.

REASONS FOR USING SOCIAL MEDIA	FACEBOOK	LINKEDIN	TWITTER	OTHER #1	OTHER #2	OTHER #3
Learn about prospects	X	X				
Research customers						
Find new employees						
Stay on top of trends						
Find my next job						
Promote my businesses						
Dating						
Be in touch with siblings						

because we can use them for these purposes doesn't mean we need to use them or should use them. You can get from New York to Los Angeles by car, train, plane, taxi, boat, or even horseback. Depending on what you are expecting to accomplish, some are much better choices than others.

Let's take our first example:

Question: What do I intend to accomplish by learning more about prospects?

Answer: I want to be better prepared before I speak with someone from one of my prospect companies, and I'd like to know more about the person I am about to call besides simply his position at his company. I'm also interested in acquaintances, experiences, and interests we may have in common.

Review your reasons for using social media that you wrote down in table 12-1 and ask yourself the question, "What do I intend to accomplish by engaging in this medium?" The answer to the question will give you insights as to whether the value you are receiving is equal to or greater than the time you are investing in it.

Step 3: Determine Your Priorities

As with everything else we want to accomplish in life, it also comes down to how great a priority it is for us and how much time we are willing to devote to it per day, week, or month. That means you have to determine social media's importance to your goals and annual accomplishments. Use table 12-2 to identify how timely and important your reasons for using social media are. You may find instances when high-importance items may not be a priority when it comes to timeliness. Choosing your priorities based on their timeliness helps in accomplishing these items first.

Step 4: Allocate Time

Just as we have a system for handling our e-mail messages, setting aside three to five times each day to read and handle our messages,

Table 12-2. Determining priorities.

REASONS FOR USING SOCIAL MEDIA	HIGH IMPORTANCE		IMPORTANT		
	TIMELY	NOT TIMELY	TIMELY	NOT TIMELY	NOT IMPORTANT
Learn about prospects					
Check out our customers					
Find new employees					
Stay on top of trends					
Find our next job opportunity					
Promote our businesses					
Dating					
Be in touch with siblings					

and a triage system for getting to the highest priority messages first, we need one for handling social media.

We recommend your social media handling system include:

- A specific number of times you set aside per day and per week
- Rules set up in Microsoft Outlook (or another e-mail and calendar program) to keep incoming social media communications out of your already overtaxed inbox
- A triage process that ensures you get to the highest-priority items first

To manage this process, we need to create Microsoft Outlook rules to either:

- Move all items from the social media service to an Outlook folder with a shortcut.
- Copy all items from this service to an Outlook folder with a shortcut depending on their importance and timeliness.

High Importance and Timely

Times should be scheduled on a routine basis to "scan for and respond to" High Importance and Timely messages. An example: If

LinkedIn and Facebook both have high importance (or important) and timely messages, set an appointment for perhaps fifteen minutes each day to:

1. Scan both folders for incoming messages.

2. Respond to the high importance and timely messages.

High Importance or Important, but Not Timely

Times should be scheduled on a routine basis to triage the messages in these folders, perhaps thirty minutes twice a week, depending on your volume, to:

1. Respond to the high importance and important messages.

2. Delete, respond to, or file the remaining messages.

3. Leave your incoming folder empty.

Figure 12-1 is an example of a scheduling system, in a weekly view.

Figure 12-1. Scheduling social media time.

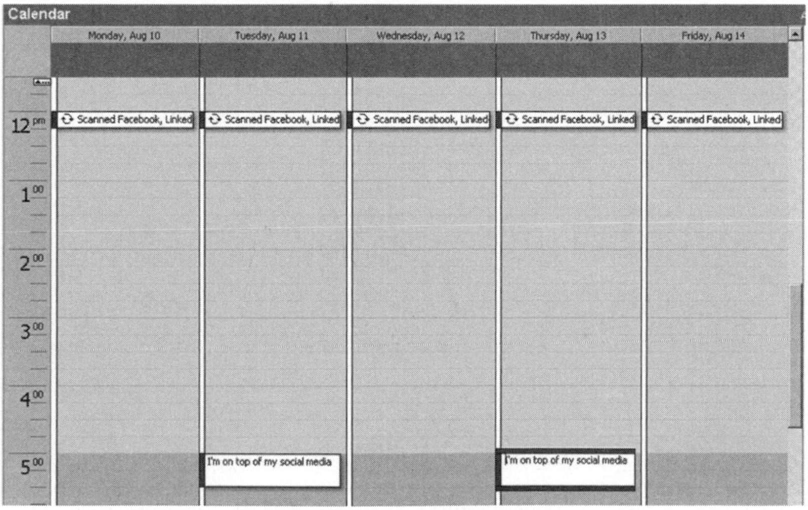

Making social media time a scheduled task in your calendar doesn't mean that you may not want to go into these folders in the evenings or on the weekends or when you need a break at other times. It just means that you can count on triaging these folders to empty them, in our example, at least twice a week. We are recommending these practices as a minimalist approach. Your actual usage depends on how much time you are willing to allocate to this effort.

For each social media service you use, you need two folders and shortcuts to these folders. As an example, for your Facebook account, you would create Facebook Incoming and Facebook Someday folders. In the same way you set up shortcuts for managing your e-mail, you can set up groups for all your different Social Media Incoming and Someday messages and then insert the shortcuts to your new folders below them. Figures 12-2 and 12-3 show how your Outlook shortcuts will look after adding these groups.

Figure 12-2. Setting up social media incoming folders.

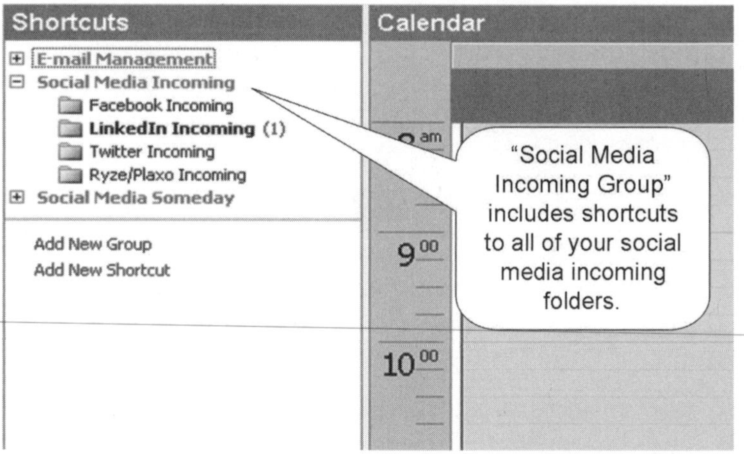

Each day when the reminder goes off on your calendar indicating it's time to scan your social media incoming folders, you simply click over to your shortcuts and open the folders. To make this task even more streamlined, we suggest you check to see if your folders are set up to indicate how many unread items they contain, rather

Figure 12-3. Setting up social media Someday folders.

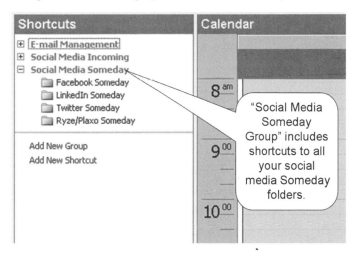

than how many total items they contain. The number will be high-lighted in blue to the right of the shortcut name. This shortcut will point you to the folders you need to scan during this brief period of time.

To create this setup, go to your Shortcut view and click on one of your new folders. Click on properties. It brings up the menu shown in figure 12-4.

Social media is here to stay. Choosing why we use it and what we want to achieve with it allows us to maximize the benefits that these technologies have to offer. It's wonderful to hear from friends, family members, and coworkers, and see their videos and view their photos and get updates on what they are up to. The downside of social media is that it can be very time-consuming. Putting systems and structures in place helps manage our usage and focus our time on what's most important.

At this point we've covered every aspect of how to organize your work and life to be more effective and get things done. You've learned how to keep your mind free from the more mundane tasks so that you can focus on those tasks and events that are most im-portant to you. You've also learned scheduling practices that allow you to design your days with intention and purpose, and create

Figure 12-4. Setting your incoming folder for new messages.

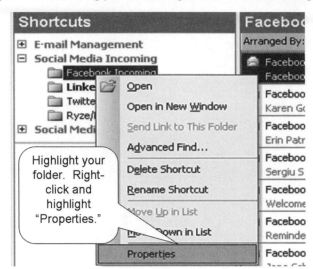

your life in a satisfying, fulfilling, and rewarding manner. Lastly, you learned how to triage your way to an empty inbox and manage your social media usage.

As you begin implementing this system, it's likely that you will encounter times when you are unable to keep some of these practices in place. When we are learning something new, it's normal that there will be setbacks along the way. Chapter 13 introduces tips and exercises on how to recover when these inevitable setbacks occur.

RELAUNCHING YOUR CREATED LIFE

Finish each day and be done with it. You have done what you could. Some blunders and absurdities have crept in; forget them as soon as you can. Tomorrow is new day. You shall begin it serenely and with too high a spirit to be encumbered with your old nonsense.

—RALPH WALDO EMERSON

This chapter is designed to help you get in touch with the resources available to you when you revert to old habits. You will learn to put yourself back in commission and back on the path of designing your days and creating your life. Perhaps you were immersed in meeting a project deadline or you returned from an illness, vacation, or other absence only to find your inbox over-loaded, your work projects piling up, and your home routine disrupted. When you are feeling demotivated, sluggish, or submerged in a sense of being overwhelmed, the simple techniques in this chapter can help you to favorably change your state of being to a state of *doing*.

The intention is for you to have a sit-down with yourself, in a gentle but intentional way, to create action again in your life. Instead of thinking, "I'll never be able to catch up; I'll never be able to start again," remember to open this chapter for inspiration and we'll take you through a step-by-step process for reentry. The goal of relaunching your productivity is to be reengaged, recommitted, and revitalized. Restart your engines!

A massage therapist once told us that people have lost touch with the healing power that we all have, especially the healing power of our hands. Whenever we stub a toe, scrape a knee, or bump our head, our first response is to put our hand over the place that hurts. For prehistoric humans, the hand was a powerful force; it was the first place to go for healing. The resources you need to heal yourself, to change yourself from disease back to ease, are already built into you (notice how, if you scrape a knee, it heals on its own without any direction from you). This chapter gives you access to your healing power, whenever you need it, to assist you in getting back on track.

BECOMING A SLUG

Is this scenario familiar? You set aside the time to do something that you've said is important to do and then you find yourself doing anything but that. You have nothing else planned, nothing that is competing for your time. You said that you would work on the monthly report and you can't even begin it. You browse the Web, check your e-mail, shuffle papers on your desk—you do anything besides beginning the report.

This is what we call becoming a slug. When you become a slug, you are alert but you find yourself doing everything you can to avoid the thing you have set out to accomplish. You probably have found yourself playing the Five More Minutes game. For example, you are lying on the couch, negotiating with yourself: "In five more minutes, I'll turn off the television and get to work." After five minutes elapse, you bargain once more: "In the next five minutes I'll begin for sure." More than thirty minutes later, you are still watching television. All the while, your stomach is churning because you know that you are not using your time the way you said you would. You've set aside the time to accomplish a task and yet here you are, squandering it.

It is something that we all do. Recognize it as a sign that perhaps something isn't working for you. Do you need a break? Are you worried or afraid of something? When you become a slug, it is often a way of dealing with stress. It is your body's way of shutting down for a little while. This is different from being exhausted, where you want to work on something but can't because of fatigue. Your eyes are closing and you can't keep them open another minute. In this instance, you need to stop and rest. Being a slug is a strategy that's used to avoid tasks we simply would rather not do.

WHO AM I?

An unknown author once wrote a riddle:

> I am your constant companion; I am your greatest helper or heaviest burden. I will push you onward or drag you down to failure. I am completely at your command. Half the things you do you might just as well turn over to me, and I will be able to do them quickly and correctly. I am easily managed—you must merely be firm with me. Show me exactly how you want something done and after a few lessons, I will do it automatically.
>
> Who am I? I am habit.

A habit is merely a familiar way of responding to a certain stimulus over and over again. When we respond to a task that makes us uncomfortable by becoming a slug, that is a habit. The good news is that habits can be changed because they are behaviorally driven, and as the previous quote suggests, habits can be "easily managed—you must merely be firm."

Once we have identified that our becoming a slug is a habit and that we are addicted to it, the question then becomes, how do we detoxify from that habit? How do we recondition our responses so that we don't become a slug every time we have to complete a task that we don't want to do?

SIX HABITS THAT KEEP US STUCK

So now you have the tools. You have created your life. You are living into it day by day, week by week, month by month. On your journey to becoming accountable to yourself by designing your days and creating your life, you are going to encounter obstacles, setbacks, and habits that can be difficult to change. When you catch yourself starting down the slippery slope of losing control of your calendar and your life, look at the habitual behaviors that are taking over.

Let's examine some of the roadblocks you may run into:

- Forgetting to take one bite at a time
- Trying to do too much too quickly
- Micromanaging the process
- Allowing the project to become an octopus
- Looking for outside motivation
- Feeling guilty about what you don't do

Take a look at this list. See if you recognize your habitual way or ways of getting stuck. Most of us have a couple of them. Once you are aware of them, you are more likely to avoid the traps.

Habit 1: Forgetting to Take One Bite at a Time

You may have heard the joke, "How do you eat an elephant?" Answer: "One bite at a time." Now, if you are like most people you've never eaten an elephant nor do you intend to. But it's a helpful anecdote. At the beginning of large projects, or even not-so-large projects, schedule the time to make your list of everything that needs to be done. On your list include the task of scheduling the time to complete or delegate each item.

When you are stuck and don't know where to begin, the key is to create momentum and take a little bite. Consult your list and choose one item that you find less daunting and complete it. Start now or schedule a specific time to begin.

Don't let the size of the project, the emotion of your day (or hour), or the condition of the office or the world be the determining factors in moving this project to completion. Eat the elephant one bite at a time.

Habit 2: Trying to Do Too Much Too Quickly

Sometimes, instead of finding yourself stuck on where to begin, you see yourself stretched and scattered in many directions. Your energy is fragmented and your progress is halted.

This habit can be hard to spot because you are running so fast you don't have time to catch yourself at it. When you find yourself trying to do too much too quickly, stop, breathe, and break down your task into manageable steps. Schedule the time to accomplish each step instead of trying to complete the entire project at once.

As human beings, our minds work much faster than our hands and our mouths. We can always come up with more things to do, say, or accomplish than there is time to complete them. We need to remind ourselves that we are indeed human, and that we have twenty-four hours a day, every day, to accomplish what we say is most important. Making sure that we've blocked time in our calendar for our routines and our appointments provides us with a more realistic view of how much time we actually have to work on tasks and projects. Letting the calendar be our guide keeps us grounded in this reality.

Habit 3: Micromanaging the Process

It is amazing how the gestation process is so passive. The mother does not have to orchestrate the process with a command such as, "Okay, cells, listen! Arm cell connect to the elbow cell!" The mother is a vessel, and the baby developing inside her is created without much direct input from the mother. She is merely the environment the baby needs to create itself.

We are struck by how this is true in so much of life. People have a tendency of wanting to force things. You believe you *have* to make them happen. However, in so many cases, all you need to do is state the intention or be clear about the outcome you want to see accomplished, and then let things take care of themselves.

Be open to the path to the results instead of managing every nook and cranny of how you get there; don't choke the creativity out of yourself. When you stop micromanaging the process and allow things to happen, the path to your goals will open wide. It's amazing what new ideas and resources "show up." The results can then be much more powerful and more effective.

Habit 4: Allowing the Project to Become an Octopus

How many times do you look at what needs to be done for a large project or an event and say, "Ugh, this thing has grown eight new arms and I can't get it all done. I don't know how to contain it."

That should sound the alarm that it's time to get clear about the desired outcomes of the project. It's time to choose what is in and out of the scope of this project. This may include renegotiating expectations with the stakeholders involved.

Habit 5: Looking for Outside Motivation

People often say, "I don't feel motivated. This project, team, and so on, doesn't do anything for me anymore. I want a pill that will make me want to complete my task." Nothing outside of you can make you want to do something, unless of course someone is threatening you with bodily harm. We think, "If I could only find that thing to keep me going, then I'd be all right." There's no need to look outside of yourself. You are all you've got. And here's the good news: That's all you need.

Motivation from the outside is short-lived. Powerful motivation comes from within. It is being clear about what is most important to *you*. It's asking yourself "Why am I doing this task in the first place?" There are two main reasons why we do or don't do things—to seek pleasure or to avoid pain. What pain does this task avoid? Or what benefit will the completion of this task provide? See if you can pinpoint the difference that doing it will make.

When you find yourself looking for motivation from outside, stop. Take the time to make the connection between the benefit you will accrue from completing the task to the task itself.

Habit 6: Feeling Guilty About What We Don't Do

After squandering time by being a slug, we are invariably late for something else because we still have to complete the tasks we've delayed doing. At this point, we may punish ourselves: "You put yourself into this predicament. You wasted that time, so you deserve to have to work late tonight. It's your fault."

There is a better way than punishing yourself. Self-degradation saps the energy and strength you need to find creative solutions and to get unstuck.

Guilt is self-indulgent. If you feel guilty about something, it allows you to feel sorry for yourself. Guilt helps you mask being responsible. "If I feel guilty and bad enough about it," you tell yourself, "then they'll feel sorry for me and lessen or change their expectations of me in some way. Maybe they'll even let me off the hook for doing what I said I would do."

We believe that if we feel guilty and, especially, if we let everybody know how guilty we feel, it will somehow make everything better. It won't. Guilt is another honorable distraction. You might even become so consumed with the guilt that now you are unable to produce what you wanted to accomplish.

Berating yourself never makes it easier to do what you've said you want to do. Be positive and remind yourself that at any time you can choose something else. Although it may not always be easy to make that choice, it is always that simple.

FIVE STEPS TO JUMP-START YOUR PRODUCTIVITY

When our actions aren't aligned with our intentions, then a breakdown in our productivity occurs. The philosopher Martin Buber said it best: "The origin of all conflict between me and my fellow men is that I do not say what I mean and that I do not do what I say."[1]

Here are five steps you can use when you find yourself misaligned and in conflict with yourself, such that you are saying one thing and yet doing something altogether different.

- Notice what you are doing without judgment.
- Name your feeling.
- Breathe.
- Know that you have a choice.
- Make a two-minute choice.

Step 1: Notice What You Are Doing Without Judgment

One of our favorite quotes says, "The range of what we think and do is limited by what we fail to notice. And because we fail to notice that we fail to notice, there is little we can do to change until we notice how failing to notice shapes our thoughts and deeds."[2]

Here is how you learn to observe yourself without judgment. The first sign of being in conflict with what you should be doing is when you feel the "warring." For most people, the warring is a physical sensation in the body. It is an acknowledgment that you aren't doing what you said you would do. It begins in the pit of your stomach; you feel nervousness and uneasiness. Then it travels to the palms of your hands, which become sweaty. At last, the struggle moves to your face, as you furrow your brow.

Then, after the warring comes the "thrashing." You tell yourself, "You're doing it again! What's wrong with you? How come you can't do what you say you're going to do? Look at you. You've squandered a half hour. You could have been done already!" Then you are so worn out by the thrashing that it fuels your case and becomes the reason you can't do it.

Be aware of how long it takes you to notice your behavior. It may take thirty or forty-five minutes before you realize that the war is raging: "Oh, yeah, that's right; I'm supposed to notice when I'm avoiding my task." The next time, your reaction time will be faster. The goal is to shorten the time it takes to notice your habit, thinking, or behavior. As soon as you recognize yours, you have a chance to make a choice.

Step 2: Name Your Feeling

Identify the feeling you are having right now. Pick two or three of the following words to describe what you are feeling: angry, sad, scared, glad, happy, optimistic, hopeful, overwhelmed, frustrated, put-upon, controlled, resentful, proud, unappreciated, worthy, unworthy, incompetent, irritated, strong, impatient, lonely, isolated, defeated.

Somebody once said that you can have your feelings but you don't have to be your feelings. You can have the feeling of being angry but you don't have to be angry. You can have the feeling of being unworthy but you don't have to be unworthy.

Next, reflect on your feeling in relation to the task you are doing. Does your feeling have anything to do with the task? Once you have separated your feeling from the task at hand, you can choose again. Let's say you name your feeling, and you are angry. Now that you know how you are feeling, you can decide whether you are committed to completing the task you set out to accomplish or whether you are committed to being angry. If you are committed to being angry, be angry. You have a choice.

Naming your feelings is a powerful act. When you name something, you neutralize the impact that it has on you. Feelings are nothing more than feelings. Not to minimize it, but sometimes when we can name and reflect on a feeling, it can create enough distance to allow us some objectivity and some flexibility, and our flexibility can get us back into action.

Step 3: Breathe

Breathing exercises are another way to bring yourself back to balance. A favorite yoga exercise is called the Breath of Joy. It is a quick and refreshing breathing exercise that instantly lifts your spirits and clears your mind of negative thoughts and tension. It oxygenates your brain and rejuvenates your body.

Here's how it works: The Breath of Joy is three inhalations taken with the arms swinging, shoulder height, forward, and then fully outstretched to the side, then extended above your head, and finishing with the arms swinging downward with the body in a slight forward crouching position. Inhale one-third of your capacity with each swing of the arms forward, to the side, and up. Then, when you drop your arms down as you bend forward at the hips and knees, exhale.

As you perform the Breath of Joy, ensure that you are taking one continuous breath in three parts, rather than three separate breathes. Exhale loudly—with a "Ha!"—when your arms are swinging downward and you are bending at the hips and knees, to allow the tension to escape from the body. Go at your own pace and if you feel dizzy, stop and sit down.

Give it a try. To begin, stand with your feet hip-width apart, knees slightly bent and arms hanging loosely by your sides. Make sure that you have enough room to swing your arms in any direction and not hit anything. Now, follow this sequence:

- Inhale, lifting your arms so they are outstretched and pointing forward, at shoulder height.
- Inhale again, and vigorously swing your arms out to your sides, shoulder height.
- Inhale once more, quickly swinging your arms up over your head.
- Bend over at the hips and let your arms swing down to hang loosely from your shoulders and exhale with a loud "Ha!"

Repeat the exercise several times. Remember, it is one continuous breath in three parts. Each swing of the arms is to be done vigorously. (For a video demonstration, go to: http://yogayak.com/2009/06/24/breath-of-joy-pranayama.)

Step 4: Know That You Have a Choice

The great thing about having choices is that as long as you are breathing, you have an endless supply of them. They don't expire or evaporate.

So you might say to yourself, "Oh, look, I noticed that I'm playing this little game with myself again, where I thrash myself for not working. I noticed it, and now I can make other choices." You might make a choice to continue doing what you are currently doing, take on the task you were avoiding, or choose something else altogether.

By choosing, you are back in control, rather than your habit controlling you. It's not only about reaching your goals; it's about living the life *you* create, including playing spider solitaire, if that strikes your fancy.

Step 5: Make a Two-Minute Choice

If you are still not ready to tackle your task, make a choice that you can live with for the next two minutes. Given the tender state that you are in at this moment, it is often best to make an initial choice that expires quickly. The goal of this short-term choice is to create movement that will get you unstuck.

For example, if you are resisting getting up from watching television to check your e-mail, tell yourself, "For two minutes, I'm going to choose to get up, sit at my desk, and answer my e-mail and after the two minutes, I can stop." You can even set a timer. By the time the timer goes off or the two minutes have expired, you have taken the action to overcome the habit and are back in control, having made a choice again.

OVERCOMING FEAR

There's a woman whose young son was afraid of monsters. There were lots of tree branches that grew outside his bedroom window, and, when the moonlight shone into his room at night, it would cast gnarled and twisted shadows on the floor. He was terrified to sleep because he knew that these shadows were dangerous monsters. One day, the boy's mother bought him a little spray bottle commonly used for houseplants and wrote "Monster Spray" in big letters across it. She gave him the bottle and practiced spraying the monsters with him. This simple little solution put him in control and gave him the power to spray the monsters away.

This chapter is your bottle of Monster Spray. Whenever you find yourself trapped by monsters (fear, procrastination, feeling inadequate), these techniques can help you get back to what you want to be doing. Using these tools, you will be able to pat that little monster and say, "Okay, go away. I know you'll be back again, but it's not your time now." The intent of overcoming the monster is to get you back to creating, to get you back in control, instead of having the monster run the show. Once you name your monster, you are back in power.

Use the Power of Fear

Years ago, I, Alesia, took a class on how to be a stand-up comic. I wasn't interested in becoming a comedienne; I wanted to learn how to bring humor into my presentations. On the last day of class, we put on a comedy show where each student performed three or four minutes of the comedy routine they had been crafting. The audience consisted of family and friends, so nobody was going to boo or throw rotten tomatoes at us. Even so, I remember being terrified right before it was my turn to go onstage. Then, when I stepped onstage, an amazing thing happened. While I was feeling the greatest amount of fear I had ever felt, I was also experiencing a new and heightened sense of aliveness that was exhilarating. I was engaged and present with the audience and had fun trying some of the jokes that I'd been collecting for use in my presentations.

Taking on things that you're afraid to do can turn out to be an enjoyable way to experience more of life.

Recognize That Fear Keeps Us Alive

We give fear too much power. The way to create more equilibrium in our relationship with fear is to first coax it out of the shadows and look at it head-on, befriend it, and allow it to do what it is designed to do: Keep us safe, alive, and present. Fear taught our earliest ancestors "fight or flight." In the present-day, fear keeps us alive in the moment and keeps us living life.

We need to transform our relationship to fear from something we deny to a source of vitality and energy. When we welcome our fear, it can become an even fuller part of our aliveness.

Create Inertia with a Gentle Choice

Newton's first law of motion (also known as the law of inertia) says that an object at rest will stay at rest, or an object in motion will stay in motion, unless acted upon by an external force. How many times have you lain in bed with a full bladder, but you don't want to get up because you're afraid you'll get cold, or that you'll wake up others, or you are afraid you won't be able to go back to sleep? You stay in bed until your bladder screams at you and forces you into action!

How do we counteract that law of inertia? How do we stay in action when we've been arrested by our fears? The first thing is to acknowledge what is going on, to admit to the fear. Once you have acknowledged the fear, you can make some simple choices that gently engage you in an activity. We often are not gentle enough with ourselves. Even a gentle action can create substantial movement.

Befriend Your Fears

Fear is going to be a constant companion. It is not going away. Fear is there to serve us by keeping us safe. It is what kept prehistoric humans alive and able to procreate. Most of their fears were physical fears, like being afraid that a tiger might jump out and eat them. These days, with all of our modern technology, most of us are not as immediately concerned with our personal safety. So, if physical risk is not an issue, what is it that we are so afraid of? Now, we are afraid of "reputational" risk. We are afraid others won't think we are smart or capable, or we are afraid that we won't be able to measure up.

We need to acknowledge that fear is a constant sidekick, and recognize that we have more power over it than we think. We can assert ourselves and lean into fear in a way that doesn't create struggle but instead creates alignment. We can ally ourselves with the fear, acknowledging that it's there and that it wants to protect us, but we can say, "I'm okay with this; you don't have to protect me. I don't need to sit here and watch TV for an hour. I know I can get up and do my taxes." Once we identify that our sidekick has come to the rescue, we can choose to tell it that we don't need it right now.

Our typical response to fear is, "What's wrong with me? I know I'm supposed to do this task and I'm not doing it. There must be something wrong with me." And there is nothing wrong with us. We need to say, "Wow, isn't this interesting? I'm noticing that I'm resisting this task. This could be a clue that I'm afraid of something."

When you first sense that you are afraid of something, tell yourself, "I'm afraid of it." Then list all the things you are afraid of. For example: "People will say it's not good enough," "I'll fail," or "I'll disappoint." Now look at what you've written and ask, "So what's the worst that can happen if all those things come about?" Chances are you won't be able to come up with a good answer. The worst that can happen is that people don't like something you did. Now think about what happened in the past when people didn't like something you did. Did you die? Were you hit with a bolt of lightning? Did you contract a terrible disease? No. Nothing life-threatening happened. You may have disappointed yourself and/or others. There may have been some unfavorable consequences, but, more than anything, you probably learned something.

You can climb down the tree a little bit, off the skinny branch, and get back to a place where you have more choices. Are you choosing to watch this television show because you enjoy it and you've allotted time to be able to watch it? Or are you watching it because you are avoiding something you are afraid of? And even if you say, "I'm choosing it because I'm avoiding or afraid of something," at least you are making a conscious choice around it. And, if it's a conscious choice, then you don't have to condemn yourself that you've done something wrong; you've decided to make this choice, and then, at any given time, instead of the choice that you've made, you can choose to make another one.

EXAMINING WHY YOU STILL "DON'T WANNA"

There will be times you "don't wanna" do something. There are always other opportunities and choices for you to make. These techniques and tools for getting you unstuck do not get you off the hook for making a choice, because when you are living your own life, you will have many choices. Life is about choosing and more choosing, from moment to moment.

A client of ours, pouting, once said, "I see a task on my calendar, but I don't want to do it." Most of us can relate to that feeling. When you don't want to do something, you forget why it shows up on your calendar in the first place. You have *forgotten* the importance. You know the task must be important or else it wouldn't be on your calendar. In the moment that you recognize you don't want to do something, you can give yourself six minutes to pout or a time-out to whine, cry, and grumble. Then ask yourself, "Why is the task on my calendar to begin with?" If doing the task won't make a difference in your life, don't do it. If it will make a difference, then figure out why you scheduled it in the first place. How important is it to you? Then do it or reschedule it.

And, if you reschedule it, you may try writing down why the task is important to you, right there with the item on your calendar. Use words that remind you why the task is important to you; later, when it is time to tackle the task, those words will be a source of inspiration to you.

Sometimes people who have been married a long time say they don't want to be married anymore. Sometimes parents say that they don't want to be a parent anymore. It is a temporary way to release tension and escape, if only for a second. Sometimes giving yourself permission to vent for a little while helps. It does not replace the need to evaluate why you are resisting something or to figure out what is important about it, but it can be a short-term relief. So decide and choose: Does the item stay on your calendar or not? If it does, why? And, most important, what is one redeeming characteristic about it that can create some movement for you?

To sum up, when you find yourself not wanting to do something that you have on your calendar:

- Give yourself the permission to whine, pout, or grumble.
- Contain your venting by giving yourself a finite amount of time; we recommend six minutes.
- Reexamine why the item is on your calendar to begin with; get back in touch with why it is important to you. Is there something that can compel you to take small steps toward doing it?
- Get back to choice mode. Is the task important enough to do? If it's not, choose not to do it. If it is, then choose when you will do it. There are consequences if you decide not to do it now. Can you live with those consequences? If not, then you need to find a time for it on your calendar.

  It might take you two, three, or four more times to schedule a task you dislike, such as filing your taxes, before you do it. Eventually, you will reach the point where the consequence of not doing the task becomes too burdensome and costly—both emotionally and, in the case of filing taxes, financially. So you *choose* to surrender, wave the white flag, give up the fight of resisting the inevitable, and you *choose* to do it yourself or have someone do it for you.

WHEN YOU STILL "DON'T WANNA" DO IT—TIPS FROM OUR CLIENTS

No one we know wants to do what he or she is supposed to do all the time. Someone who did would be a robot. We have given you some suggestions, some questions, and some exercises to use when you don't feel like doing a task. Since this condition of "don't wanna" will be with us for the rest of our lives, here are a few more suggestions from our clients.

Mike, a successful small-business owner who has created a wonderful life for himself, his family, his employees, his church, and his community, says: "When all else fails, what works best for me, and I hate to say it, is to lose the time to choose. I wait until there is no time left to change course, no time left to delegate, no time left to renege on my commitment, and then I cry uncle and just do it."

Evan, a manager in a software development company, suggests: "What I've found most useful is making sure I set my day up to be realistic. By realistic I mean allowing for my routines, including interruptions and emergencies, and not just what I want my day to look like. In setting my days up this way, I can shortstop the 'I don't wannas' before they happen. And what I'm finding is that, when they do happen, it's usually when I wing it and don't realistically schedule my day."

Jenna, an executive with a biotech company, offers this suggestion: "The real power in handling the 'I don't wannas' is in learning to say no. Now that I am designing my days and weeks, scheduling the work I intend to accomplish, I have a much clearer picture of my life and my commitments. Now that I can be honest with myself, I find it much easier to say no to certain requests made of me that I would not have been able to say no to before."

WHEN ALL ELSE FAILS

Setbacks are recognized as a standard part of engaging in new practices or learning new habits. In the book *Changing for Good*,[3] the authors studied thousands of individuals confronting long-standing and difficult problems. They found that only 20 percent of people are able to change their behavior on the first try. Most people should expect and prepare for setbacks. Relapse is most often caused by emotional stress. When emotions get out of order, it is common to revert to old and more comfortable ways of behaving. Many times people will experience frustration as they try something new and say it's too hard and give up. Besides emotional turmoil, lapses in environmental management contribute most often to setbacks.[4] For example, you acquire the habit of capturing everything in your preferred capture tool (i.e., your BlackBerry or a plain old notepad), whereas before you'd jot notes on Post-its. You fill up your capture tool and in a pinch start using the Post-it notes again. After a week you are back to having everything scattered on various Post-it notes.

The opposite of excusing a small indiscretion is to overreact to one small slip. If you do momentarily relapse and give in to an old habit, it doesn't mean you've failed. Get back on track again.

The difficulty with a relapse is the negative emotions that are generated. Feelings of failure, discouragement, and demoralization can occur. When relapse happens, complete failure is rarely the result. It isn't likely that you will need to start over from the beginning. Just start where you left off and get into action.

It is important to extract the benefits of relapse. Learn why you slipped. Then be conscious of these pitfalls. You can profitably build prevention into your next plan of action.

When all else fails, here are some surefire strategies to get you back in action. The following Inaction Antidotes are sure to cure what ails you. Try them out and have fun with them. They are simple but powerful exercises that generate energy and forward momentum. Don't take our word for it, see for yourself.

Inaction Antidote 1: Take It or Leave It

When you find yourself avoiding a task, take a step back and choose whether you will or will not do it. And clearly articulate the reasons why or why not. Use the "take it or leave it" decision tree to help you.

1. Make a list of things that you don't want to do, but you know are important to do.

2. Select an item from the list you created in step 1. For sixty seconds, whine and grumble about why you don't want to do it. Really get into it, with great emotion and affect.

3. Revisit the item and get back in touch with why it is important to you. Write down its importance.

Table 13-1. Inaction antidote 1: Take it or leave it.

NO, I WON'T DO IT.	YES, I WILL DO IT.
a. What are the consequences of this choice?	c. What are the consequences of this choice?
b. Can you live with these consequences? Yes—cross off or delete it! No—continue to c. in the next column.	d. Write something that can compel you to take small steps toward doing it.
	e. Choose a time(s) in your calendar to complete the item.

4. Get back to choice mode. Is the task important enough to do? Use table 3-1 to test your choice.

Inaction Antidote 2: Action Algorithm

Another approach to consider when you find yourself unable to get started is the action algorithm. Often when you can identify what you want to accomplish (as a result of doing something) you can create momentum and energy to take action. Answering the questions listed in table 13-2 can help you get to the source of what you want to accomplish and can catapult you into action.

Inaction Antidote 3: Setting the Scene for Action

What are the conditions that will compel, entice, invite, and encourage you to engage in what you want to accomplish? What are the environmental elements that increase the likelihood for you to take action? Setting yourself up for success means creating an environment that nurtures and supports your creativity and productivity. Review the list of environmental factors in table 13-3 and check off the items that you find pleasing and add items that are missing. Then see what changes you can make to your surroundings that will make it easier for you to get in action.

Also, consider the effect of food on your mood. Are you sluggish

Table 13-2. Inaction antidote 2: Action algorithm.

QUESTION	YOUR RESPONSE
What will you accomplish by completing this item/task?	
Why is it important to accomplish it?	
How will you feel upon completing the task/item?	
What will you need to do? What are the discrete steps required to accomplish this item? How much time might each step take?	
What materials or information will you need to complete this task/item? Collect the materials/information now or schedule a time to do so.	
How will you reward yourself for completing this item?	
What will you accomplish by completing this item/task?	
Why is it important to accomplish it?	
How will you feel upon completing the task/item?	

after lunch? Do you experience a sugar crash in the afternoon? Can't function without caffeine in the morning? What adjustments might you make?

Inaction Antidote 4: When, Then Planning Scenarios

Use table 13-4 for the final exercise, where you answer the following questions: What are some "likely" scenarios that may prevent you from being successful with implementing these new practices, and how can you address them?

Table 13-3. Inaction antidote 3: Setting the scene for action.

SENSE	ENVIRONMENTAL ELEMENTS	
See	☐ Outside view ☐ Plants or flowers nearby ☐ Mini-waterfall ☐	☐ Soft lighting ☐ A clear and organized workspace ☐
Hear	☐ Music type: _____ ☐	☐ White Noise ☐
Smell	☐ Scented candles ☐ Scent diffuser ☐	☐ Fragrance sprayed in the room ☐ Potpourri ☐
Touch	☐ Squeezable toys ☐ Ball that can be tossed ☐ Pen or other object to twirl ☐	☐ Chair comfort ☐ Desk and computer monitor ergonomic situation ☐
Taste	☐ Mints ☐ Chocolates ☐ Chewing gum ☐ Candy ☐	☐ Fruits and vegetables ☐ Popcorn ☐ Snacks ☐ Cookies ☐
Time	☐ Early morning ☐ Late morning ☐ Early afternoon	☐ Late afternoon ☐ Early evening ☐ Late evening
	* Most focused and energetic	X Most distracted and tired

OVERCOMING INERTIA

Action produces results in our physical world. Thoughts alone won't. Intentions alone won't. Faith alone won't. Only action will. Sometimes we need to coax ourselves into action or ease ourselves into it. Use these "Inaction Antidotes" whenever you need a little push to get you moving, because once you start moving, it's easier to stay in motion.

Table 13-4. Inaction antidote 4: When, then planning.

CONDITIONS	PREVENTIONS AND INTERVENTIONS
List what is likely to occur that could cause a relapse or setback with these new practices:	I can engage it to minimize or prevent relapse/breakdowns from occurring:

Fill in the sentences below:

When I _____, then I'll _____ to get back on track.

When I _____, then I'll _____ to get back on track.

When I _____, then I'll _____ to get back on track.

When I _____, then I'll _____ to get back on track.

14

PARTING WORDS

*Success is not final, failure is not fatal. It is the courage to
continue that counts.*

—*WINSTON CHURCHILL*

Our hope for you is that this book provides some effective
methods to deal with the madness of modern-day living so that
you can create more time for you to do the things in life that are
fulfilling and rewarding while having peace of mind that you have
everything under control.

The onslaught of information that bombards us on a daily basis
is unprecedented in human history. The expectation to synthesize,
manage, respond, and use the data is also unparalleled. Our wish is
that you have new ways of processing and handling everything that
comes at you in your life. Although this is the end of the book, it is
the beginning of you being more effective and productive by practicing these tools that will support you.

You will be clearer on what's most important by creating your
life through accomplishments and then living into the accomplishments you've created. You've learned how to triage your capture
tool and mange your e-mail and social media. You now know how
to design your days, weeks, and months according to your plan and
your wishes.

Here are a few final thoughts we would like to leave you with to remember what is most important about living this new life you've created.

• *Keep your accomplishments in the forefront.* You took the time and the energy to create your accomplishments. Embrace and keep them in front of you. Use them. Read through each realm of your life that you created. Visualize your success: how you will feel, where you will be, and what you will be doing. Your accomplishments tell you what the endgame is by defining what it means to win in your life, what it looks and feels like, so you'll recognize your success.

• *Be ready.* Be aware and ready for change. Know what you want and what's important so you can change in a flash. Tennis players bounce on the balls of their feet waiting for the serve, so they are ready to go in any direction the second the ball comes over the net. Be present in your life today. Keep yourself ready and open to accept the opportunities that come your way.

Stay present to what's important to you and what you want in life, because you need to be able to pull in resources that are out there waiting to line up and deliver for you.

• *Be the star in your life.* Our lives can be distilled to to-do lists, and we can see ourselves as automatons with tasks to complete. It's easy for life to dissolve to that state, yet there is so much more to be had through intentionally creating your life. In this fast-paced, turbocharged world, it's easy to be disconnected from the power that you have to orchestrate your life.

Ask yourself, "Am I the star in my life?" Don't play a supporting role—take the lead. When you create your annual accomplishments, you write the script and have a big say in how your life goes. Once you've created it, there's no one else who can live that life but you. Step into life and appreciate what a privilege it is to determine what your life will be. Design your life and live it according to what you say is important, according to the contributions that you want to make, and according to what is going to fulfill you.

Be gentle with yourself as you take on these practices. If on your way you have questions, experiences, or thoughts you want to express to others who have read or will read this book, we invite you to share them at www.moretimeforyou.2beffective.com.

Appendix A
IMPLEMENTATION
ACTION PLAN

This appendix contains a series of checklists for implementing the *More Time for You* system. We call it our Four-Week Implementation Action Plan to help you apply the key practices recommended in this book. Be sure to schedule time in your calendar to review each of these items over the next four weeks.

Table A-1. Week one implementation action plan.

WEEK 1 ACTIVITIES	
	1. Choose a primary capture device.
	2. Set up your Outlook folders and/or shortcuts.
	3. Review and practice the triage method for emptying your capture device.
	4. Empty your inbox and practice your e-mail and social media triage each day.
	5. Continue writing your Annual Accomplishments.
	6. Conduct your weekly review.
	7. Celebrate your progress.

Table A-2. Week two implementation action plan.

WEEK 2 ACTIVITIES
1. Look at areas where you procrastinated or weren't able to accomplish what you wanted; apply one of the Inaction Antidotes to create movement.
2. Make a list of your daily, weekly, monthly, and quarterly routines, then schedule them in your calendar.
3. If you are concerned about the messages in your Freedom folder, schedule a time each week to view them.
4. Check your Waiting for Response folder each day.
5. Continue to triage your capture device, e-mail, and social media.
6. Conduct a weekly review.
7. Celebrate your progress.

Table A-3. Week three implementation action plan.

WEEK 3 ACTIVITIES
1. Practice saying no.
2. Look at how often you are "moving" or "rescheduling" certain activities. Reconsider what you want to do with them.
3. Create some e-mail rules for assisting you in emptying your inbox each day.
4. Share your Annual Accomplishments with someone.
5. Continue to triage your capture device, e-mail, and social media.
6. Check your Waiting for Response folder each day.
7. Conduct a weekly review.
8. Celebrate your progress.

Table A-4. Week four implementation action plan.

WEEK 4 ACTIVITIES	
	1. Have you scheduled enough time for interruptions and distractions each day? If not, schedule more.
	2. Schedule a project using a checklist.
	3. Utilize another Inaction Antidote when you find you are stuck or suffering a setback.
	4. Create some e-mail rules for assisting you in emptying your Inbox each day.
	5. Continue to triage your capture device, your e-mail, and social media.
	6. Share your Annual Accomplishments with someone.
	7. Check your Waiting for Response folder each day.
	8. Conduct a weekly review.
	9. Celebrate your progress.

Appendix B
ADDITIONAL TECHNIQUES FOR MANAGING CALENDAR AND E-MAIL SYSTEMS

This appendix provides additional instructions on many of the various scheduling techniques intended to assist you in streamlining your work. Use this material alongside the information in previous chapters (especially chapters 5 through 10) and appendix A, our Four-Week Implementation Action Plan. We used Microsoft Outlook versions 2003 and 2007 in the screenshots used as illustrations throughout the book. Any instructions can be implemented in both versions.

1. Setting Up Your Shortcut View

2. Setting Up Shortcuts to Streamline Handling a High Volume of E-Mail Messages

3. Setting Up Your Inbox View

4. Setting Up Your Waiting for Response Folder View

5. Setting Up the Someday Folder View

6. Adding a Calendar Shortcut to Your Shortcut Bar

7. Moving an E-Mail Message to Your Calendar

8. Setting Up Shortcuts to Streamline Communications with People You Interact with Frequently

9. Creating Shortcuts for Active Projects

10. Creating a Copy Rule

SETTING UP YOUR SHORTCUT VIEW

Using the Shortcut Bar in Microsoft Outlook allows you to keep active and important folders at your fingertips without the need to dig through your personal folders. It is the recommended method for individuals receiving hundreds of messages each day and individuals who manage multiple people or multiple projects at a time.

To begin, open your Shortcut Bar by accessing it from your Navigation Pane. It is shown by the arrow icon (see figure B-1).

Your shortcut view may have preexisting shortcuts in it, such

Figure B-1. Shortcut bar and icon.

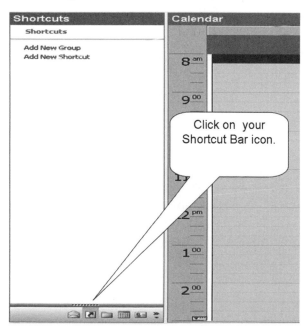

as "Outlook Today" or others. Begin by deleting all existing shortcuts (figure B-2). Right-click on the shortcut, then choose "Delete Shortcut" from the pull-down menu, highlight it, and click "Yes" when it asks if you want to delete the existing shortcut.

Figure B-2. Deleting preexisting shortcuts.

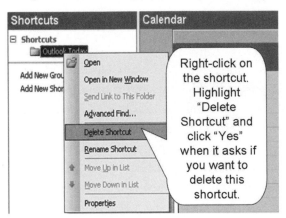

There is no need to worry about this information disappearing. This is merely a shortcut to get to your folder, which is securely saved in your personal folders. Continue deleting until you have an empty Shortcut Bar. If you previously set up the Waiting for Response and Someday shortcuts, you do not need to delete them.

SETTING UP YOUR E-MAIL SHORTCUTS

When you receive a large volume of e-mail messages each day, you may want to set up a group in your shortcuts to aid in getting your inbox to zero. To begin create a "New Group" and label it "E-mail Management" (figure B-3). Click on "New Group" and it creates a new group that is highlighted, ready for you to type in the label "E-mail Management."

You will set up shortcuts for each of your e-mail folders. Click on "Add New Shortcut." It opens your "Personal Folders" (figure B-4).

Figure B-3. Creating your E-Mail Management Group.

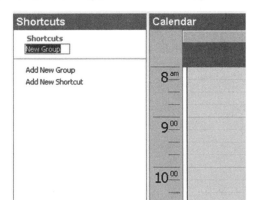

Figure B-4. Adding an e-mail shortcut.

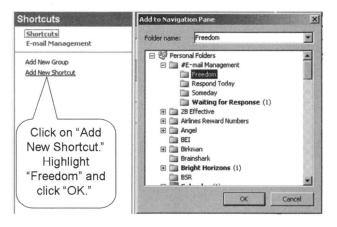

Repeat this process for the following folders:

Respond Today
Someday
Waiting for Response
Inbox
Sent Items

Your Shortcut View will look as shown in figure B-5 when complete.

Figure B-5. E-Mail Management Shortcuts.

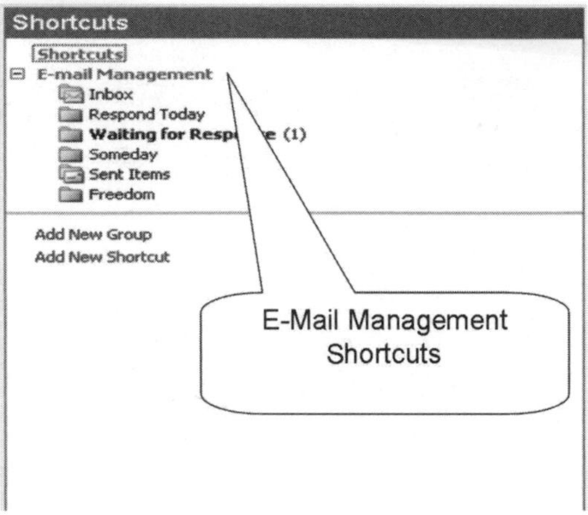

If the E-mail Shortcuts appear above the E-mail Management Group, simply drag them below it.

SETTING UP YOUR INBOX VIEW

When you use the "Messages" view for your inbox, you can preview much of the e-mail message without actually opening it. You might find that making triage decisions are easier with this broader view of your e-mail messages.

Figure B-6 shows how to set up your inbox with the "Messages" view. From the Microsoft Outlook toolbar:

1. Choose the "View" tab.

2. Select "Arrange By."

3. Select "Current View."

4. Then select the box next to "Messages" view.

Figure B-6. Setting up your inbox view.

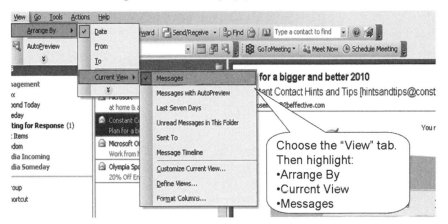

Figure B-7. Messages view.

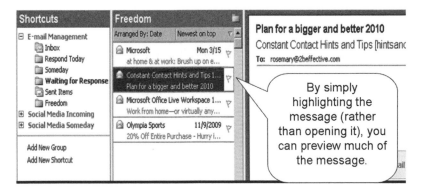

Your inbox view will look like the screen shown in figure B-7.

The advantage of the Messages view is it allows you to view the message at a glance to quickly determine how to handle each incoming e-mail. There is often no need to open the entire message; you have enough information in the message pane to make your triage decision to either:

- Delete it.
- Do it.
- File it.

Then, it's a simple matter of deleting, doing, or dragging the message to the appropriate folder. When you drag the items from your inbox to one of your e-mail folders, they leave your inbox.

SETTING UP YOUR WAITING FOR RESPONSE FOLDER VIEW

When you use the "Messages with AutoPreview" view, your messages appear as a list that can be sorted, arranged, and color-coded in a manner that allows you to view the contents quickly, which is particularly useful when reviewing your Waiting for Response folder at the end of the day.

Figure B-8 shows how to set up this view. From the Outlook toolbar:

Figure B-8. Messages with AutoPreview view.

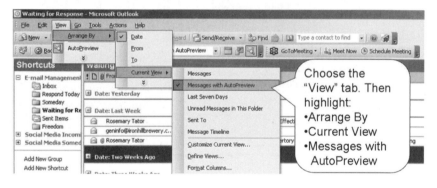

1. Choose the "View" tab.

2. Select "Arrange By."

3. Select "Current View."

4. Then select the box next to "Messages with AutoPreview."

Your Waiting for Response folder view will look like the screen shown in figure B-9. Now you can view the subject line of the messages at a glance. During your review of this folder at the end of the day, you will be able to determine how to handle each message or note that you posted. Once again, you can:

- Delete it. You have received the information you were waiting for.
- Do it. You still haven't received the information, so take action and either call the person, send another message, or stop by their office to remind them.
- Leave it for another day. It's not critical that you have the information today and you can count on yourself to review this folder again tomorrow, when you can make new decisions on the message.

Figure B-9   Waiting for Response folder view.

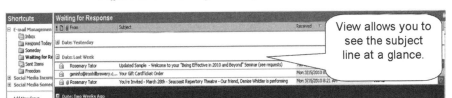

Using the "Colored Flags" in Your Folders

Once you start using your Waiting for Response folder on a daily basis, you may have a dozen or more items in here. Using colored flags to categorize these items allows you to see at a glance what you need to attend to. Open your folder and right-click on the flag icon on your first message. It brings up a menu, as shown in figure B-10.

There are many different ways to color-code your messages. You can assign specific colors for messages from family, clients, current project(s), and organizations where you may volunteer. You can choose to "flag" the message or not. When you do "flag" the message, you can have your messages sorted (figure B-11), by color or category, seeing all messages for which you are waiting for a response from someone. Simply click on the flag icon and they will be sorted by color.

When you post notes to your Waiting for Response folder or drag e-mail messages here and color-code them, you can see them

Figure B-10. Adding flags to waiting for response.

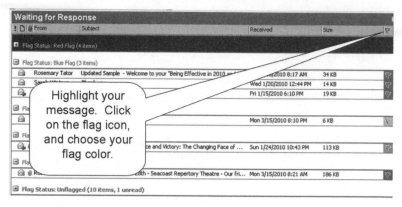

Figure B-11. Using flags to sort "Waiting for Response" messages.

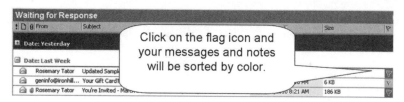

at a glance and handle them effectively. Items in this folder need to be viewed at least once a day, since they are things you are committed to doing or handling.

SETTING UP THE SOMEDAY FOLDER VIEW

This is another folder where it is simpler to view the contents in a "list view" rather than one message at a time. Use the same setup instructions as with your Waiting for Response folder and your Someday folder will look like the screen shown in figure B-12.

You can choose to "flag" the message or not. You can choose to use your colors in a variety of ways for categorizing. One method is

Figure B-12. Someday folder view.

E-mail messages and posted notes in your Someday folder, flagged together by color.

to color-code by the realms of your life, which you set up in chapter 5. Then, when you do "flag" the message, you can have your messages sorted by color, seeing all messages related to one realm of your life at a time.

ADDING YOUR CALENDAR ICON TO YOUR SHORTCUT VIEW

When you are triaging your e-mail messages, you may often find that you want to schedule a specific time in your calendar to work on them. To make this process as streamlined as possible, we recommend you add your calendar to your Shortcut View. Figure B-13 shows how to create a calendar shortcut.

If you have decided that you need a block of time to work on your response to a message and want to schedule it in your calendar, simply drag the message to your calendar folder.

See figure B-14.

Highlight the message you want to create time to handle. Left-click and drag it into your calendar shortcut. It takes the information and fills in a calendar entry for you (see figure B-4). This saves you from having to retype and insert the message yourself. It will be done automatically. All you need to do now is to adjust the date

Figure B-13. Adding your calendar to your Shortcut View.

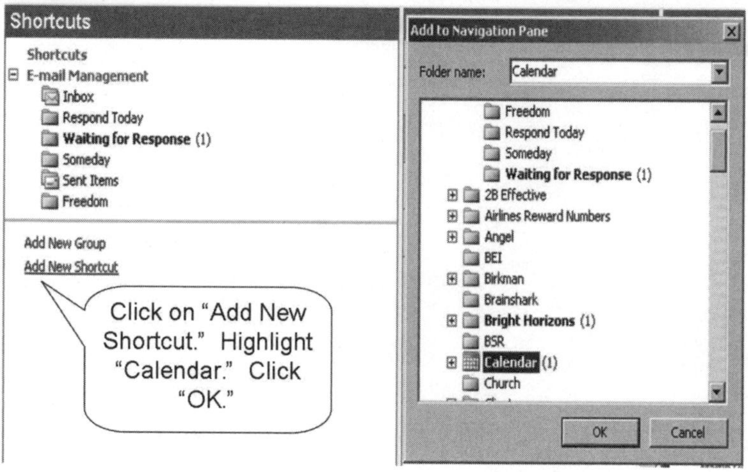

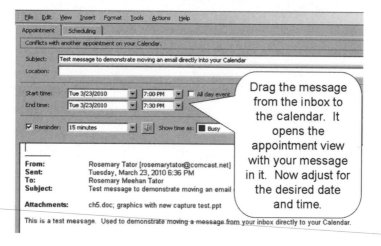

Figure B-14. Adding your calendar to your Shortcut View.

and time to fit your needs. The program's default is today's date and the current time.

This feature allows you to handle the message with a couple clicks and keeps you focused on triaging your e-mail and emptying your inbox. It's one more way to set yourself up to keep distractions to a minimum and stay focused on what you've chosen to do.

CREATING SHORTCUTS TO STREAMLINE COMMUNICATIONS WITH PEOPLE YOU INTERACT WITH FREQUENTLY

Previously in this appendix we set up a shortcut for your calendar to make it simpler to drag messages from your inbox to your calendar. Now we'll suggest a few other uses for groups and shortcuts.

For people you interact with frequently, such as staff members, you may want to have quick access to their folders. You may also want to keep a copy of all their communications. Set up a group (e.g., My Staff) with several shortcuts to their e-mail folders. Use the same process you used for setting up your E-mail Management group and shortcuts. Figure B-15 is an example of how this setup looks.

Figure B-15. Creating shortcuts to streamline communications with key people.

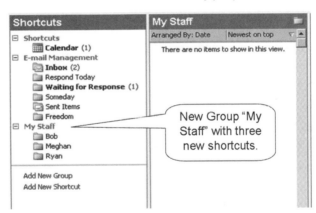

Setting up these folders to use the "Messages with AutoPreview" view allows you to use this folder for several purposes:

1. Keep a copy of all messages that come from these key contacts (you may even want to create a copy rule, so that whenever you get a message from these people a copy of the message automatically goes to this folder; see instructions later in this appendix).

2. Store all incoming and outgoing messages from your key contacts,

so it's simpler to go back and locate a specific message or check to see if you actually sent something to them.

3. Post notes and drag messages into this folder that you want to discuss at your next one-on-one meeting or group meeting. Using the folder in this manner greatly cuts down on interruptions caused by your having to dash off another e-mail, send another voice message, or stop people in the hall. It also decreases the e-mail and voice mail traffic between you and each of your key contacts. If you are using this folder for this purpose, we recommend you choose a color-coding scheme and code all messages you want to discuss with them so they are easily distinguishable from other messages and notes you are just saving. Once you've discussed them, you could delete them or change their color to denote that the item or message has been handled.

CREATING SHORTCUTS FOR ACTIVE PROJECTS

For active projects, where you have frequent messages and want to make sure you have fast access to the project folders, set up shortcuts as well. Start by setting up a Project group and then create shortcuts to the e-mail folders for each of the projects you want to include in your Shortcut Bar (see figure B-16).

Another useful way to manage projects is to keep relevant documents that you need to access frequently during the day on your Shortcut Bar next to your project e-mail folder. These documents may be Word documents, Excel spreadsheets, PowerPoint presentations, or PDF files.

To do this, open the folder with the document for which you want a shortcut. Highlight the document. Then carefully drag that file over to your Shortcut Bar. This may not work the first time. It can be a little "finicky." Figure B-17 shows how this setup looks in the end.

To stay focused and avoid being distracted, be sure to close the groups of shortcuts you are not using.

Figure B-16. Creating shortcuts for active projects.

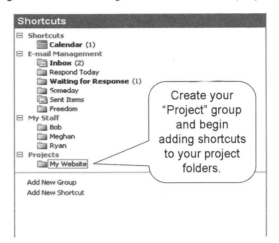

Figure B-17. Creating shortcuts for important documents
for active projects.

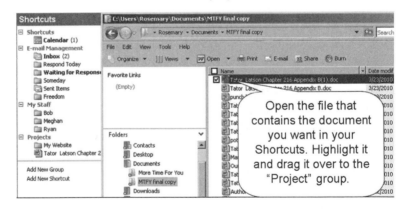

CREATING A COPY RULE

The process is similar to the one used in chapter 10 to create the delete rule.

Select Tools on the Microsoft Outlook toolbar and from the drop-down menu choose "Rules and Alerts" and then "New Rule." Instead of choosing the button next to "Start from a template," choose "Start from a blank rule" and click "Next" (figure B-18).

Figure B-18. Creating a rule for copying to a specified folder.

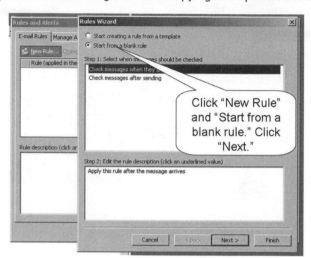

This brings up the Rules Wizard, under Step 1, choose from people or distribution list. Under step 2, click on "people or distribution list" (figure B-19).

This brings you to your Contacts. Highlight the e-mail address

Figure B-19. Creating a rule for copying to a specified folder.

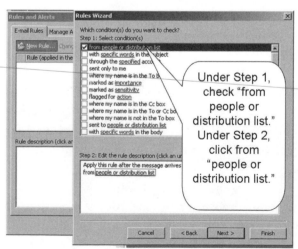

of the person or distribution list whose messages you want automatically copied to a specific folder. Click "From" and "OK." And "Next" (figure B-20).

Figure B-20. Creating a rule for copying to a specified folder.

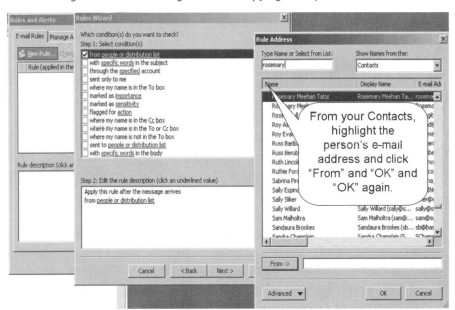

This brings up the Rules Wizard again. Under Step 1, check off "move a copy to the specified folder." Under Step 2, click on "specified folder."

This brings you to your e-mail folders. Choose the folder (or create a new folder) you want messages from this person to be sent to automatically (figure B-21).

At this point your rule is essentially complete. Review your results in Step 2. If correct, click on "Finish" (figure B-22) and Outlook will make a name for the rule you just created. You can later "rename" it if you wish. Or you can continue through the next several screens by clicking "Next."

Figure B-21. Creating a rule for copying to a specified folder.

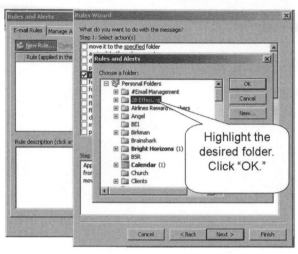

Figure B-22. Creating a rule for copying to a specified folder.

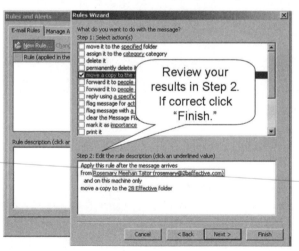

NOTES

CHAPTER 1

1. Jack Canfield, *The Success Principles* (New York: HarperCollins, 2004), 229.
2. George Leonard, *Mastery: The Keys to Long-Term Success and Fulfillment* (New York: Dutton, 1991), 15.

CHAPTER 2

1. Danny Rocks, "What Is Your Speaking Rate?" www.thecompanyrocks.com/blog/2008/04/10/what-is-your-speaking-rate/ (accessed August 11, 2008).
2. Arien Mack and Irvin Rock, *Inattentional Blindness* (Cambridge: MIT Press, 1998).

CHAPTER 3

1. Albert Einstein, *Quote DB*, www.quotedb.com/quotes/14 (accessed October 28, 2009).
2. Edward T. Hall, *The Silent Language* (New York: Anchor Books, 1973).
3. Peter M. Senge, *The Fifth Discipline: The Art & Practice of the Learning Organization* (New York: Currency Doubleday, 2006), and MindSpring, "Ladder of Inference," http://mindspring.wordpress.com/2008/01/20/ladder-of-inference/ (accessed August 11, 2008).

CHAPTER 4

1. Heike Bruch and Sumantra Ghoshal, "Beware the Busy Manager," *Harvard Business Review,* February 2002.

CHAPTER 5

1. Debra Lund, "FranklinCovey Survey Reveals Top 3 New Year's Resolutions for 2008," Reuters, December 18, 2007, http://www.reuters.com/article/pressRelease/idUS132935 + 18-Dec-2007 + BW20071218 (accessed August 12, 2008).

CHAPTER 6

1. Edward M. Hallowell, *CrazyBusy* (New York: Ballantine Books, 2006).
2. Charlie Greer, "What Are You Thinking? Part Deux," http://www.hvac profitboosters.com/Tips/Tip_Archive/tip_archive7.html (accessed August 12, 2008).

CHAPTER 8

1. William Ury, *The Power of a Positive No* (New York: Bantam Books, 2007), 133.

CHAPTER 9

1. "Spunlogic Hosts E-mail Psychology Seminar," eMedia Wire, http://www .emediawire.com/releases/2005/4/emw228155.htm (accessed August 12, 2008).

CHAPTER 11

1. Justin Kruger et al., "Egocentrism over E-mail: Can We Communicate as Well as We Think?" *Journal of Personality and Social Psychology* 89, no. 6 (December 2005): 925–936.

CHAPTER 12

1. "Global Faces and Networked Places: A Nielsen Report on Social Networking's New Global Footprint," March 2009, http://mashable.com/2009/03/09/social-networking-more-popular-than-email/ (accessed October 28, 2009).
2. Erik Qualman, "Social Media: Fad or Revolution?" *Search Engine Watch*, www .searchenginewatch.com http://searchenginewatch.com/3634651 (accessed October 28, 2009).

CHAPTER 13

1. Martin Buber, *The Way of Man: According to the Teaching of Hasidism* (New York: Citadel Press, 1966).
2. Daniel Goleman, *Vital Lies, Simple Truths* (New York: Simon & Schuster, 1985).
3. J. O. Prochaska, J. C. Norcross, and C. C. DiClemente, *Changing for Good* (New York: William Morrow, 1994).
4. James Clairborn and Cherry Pedrick, *The Habit Change Workbook: How to Break Bad Habits and Form Good Ones* (Oakland, CA: New Harbinger, 2001), 108.

INDEX

About the Authors

Rosemary Meehan Tator, principal partner of 2beffective™ LLC, provides clients with the keys to increasing their effectiveness while reducing stress. A management consultant, serial entrepreneur, coach, and motivational speaker for over 25 years, she provides leadership development programs as well as productivity, effectiveness, and sales training programs, including web-based modules, throughout the U.S. and Europe. Her clients include AT&T, IHS, Bright Horizons, SolidWorks, and major financial services companies. Her unique approach quickly moves individuals and groups to higher levels of performance, providing them insights and tools to recognize their unique talents and realize their full potential. Some of the firms she has launched include:

• GreenPages, Inc., a corporate computer value-added reseller. Co-founder and VP of Sales and Marketing, she was responsible for building the team that grew the company at over 100 percent a year for five years in a row, to $100 million in sales and thirty-six on the INC 500 list.

• Avalon Solutions, Inc., a computer solutions provider. As president and CEO, she grew the company $8 million + in sales in two years, reaching number 62 on the Dun & Bradstreet/*Entrepreneur*'s "Hot 100 Companies" list.

Rosemary is a certified professional in many disciplines, including Mission Control Productivity, the Birkman Assessment Method, Spiral Dynamics, Adizes Institute Management and Leadership, Miller Heisman's Strategic Selling, as well as certifying other leaders for Mission Control. She lives with her husband, Wes, in Dover, NH. Contact her at info@2beffective.com.

Alesia Latson, as principal of the Latson Leadership Group, has been studying and practicing the art and science of leadership and organizational development for over twenty years. She has held management and organizational development roles in Fortune 100 financial services organizations and healthcare. Through expert facilitation and personal coaching, she has developed hundreds of leaders at all levels to expand their productivity, management, and leadership impact. She is appreciated for her insight, creativity, and her exceptional skills as a consultant, executive coach, and speaker.

Ms. Latson received her M.A. in Training and Organizational Development from Lesley University and her B.A. from the University of Illinois. Formerly an adjunct faculty member of Lesley University and Bentley College, she is a frequent guest speaker at Babson Executive Education, MIT Sloan School of Business, and the University of Michigan's Ross Business School. She lives with her husband, Brian, in Sharon, MA. Contact her at info@2beffective.com.

(Continued from page ii)

"Since being introduced to the principles and practices in *More Time for You* I am acutely aware of how I spend my time; no more wasted time spent on 'obligatory meetings.' I have found that once you are being truly present, dedicated, purposeful, effective, and efficient, the results are so great, there is no turning back."—G.E.M. (Trudy) van den Berg, President, 2bcoaching , The Netherlands

"[T]he definitive book for the busy person or executive to help streamline their everyday workload. *More Time for You* is filled with practical ways to increase your productivity, tips to organize and prioritize your work day through the effective use of calendars and efficient time savers, and powerful ways to get control of your e-mail inbox immediately. I highly recommend this book as an effective tool to increase your output and capacity in an easy, stress-free manner!"—Lois Matheson, Business Counselor, Women's Business Center, Portsmouth, NH

"I have all too often found myself buying into the notion that knowing equals doing. Rosemary Tator and Alesia Latson offer excellent, practical tools for closing the gap between identifying and actually realizing what is truly important."—Jamie Kistler, RN, Owner/Health Educator, Weigh Ahead LLC

"The book's down-to-earth examples inspired me to have a fresh look at my own productivity habits. I've seen a noticeable increase in my effectiveness and productivity."—Eb Schmidt, President, Productivity 21 LLC

"The systems in *More Time for You* have provided me with a simple yet highly effective way to keep my fast-paced career and family life in order. As a working mother with pre-school twin daughters, I appreciate having a system that incorporates all of my life—and being present with what's at hand at any given time."—Kristi Scarpone, M.Ed., Fundraising Consultant

"Of the many insightful and useful practices in *More Time for You*, creating annual accomplishments has altered my life. I work from my home and these systems have given my office the kind of structure I could never seem to put in place on my own. Now I know where everything is and I love the feeling of 'nothing left to do or handle.' Whenever things begin to pile up, I know exactly what to do. My life is in order, from the biggest plans and dreams down to the smallest receipts or business cards. This makes each day pressure-free and enables me to truly enjoy my work. Thank you, for the revolutionary idea that things can get done in an atmosphere of ease, grace, and peace of mind."—Carol Dearborn, author and artist

"This is a valuable work, and I recommend it to every executive looking to improve their time management skills within their organizations as well as have satisfied employees."—Cathleen M. Moynihan, Senior Account Executive, The SAVO Group

"In *More Time for You,* Tator and Latson provide a state-of-the-art technology for the average person, seasoned professionals, top executives, and anyone who wants greater effectiveness to translate their life's visions into concrete and satisfying accomplishments."—Andrew L. Miser, Ph.D., Professional Coach, Elysian Enterprises